CHILTON'S MODERN BOATING GUIDE SERIES

Under the Advisory Editorship of Hank Wieand Bowman

Guide to Sailing

LEONARD M. FOWLE

*Photograph on Cover Courtesy of Miami, Florida,
News Bureau*

CHILTON COMPANY — BOOK DIVISION

Publishers

Philadelphia   New York

Contents

Introduction

This book is designed to interest (nay, to entice!) the uninitiated into sailing boats—although the author hopes many experienced sailors will find its pages worthwhile. To accomplish this, it is necessary first to acquaint the beginner with the joys of sailing, and to introduce him to certain nautical terms and the three principal components of a boat—hull, sails, and rigging.

Next, an understanding must be given of what makes a boat go and how she is handled on various points of sailing. This book will permit the novice to be completely self-taught, if necessary, although some practical demonstration and instruction by experienced sailors to supplement "book larnin'" is recommended—in fact, strongly advised. As in any sport, practice makes perfect, and here, most certainly, practice is necessary to any degree of skill. With this book as a guide, the novice can start sailing single-handed very soon.

There is more to sailing than simply the ability to beat to windward, reach, and run, with a fair degree of competence. One must learn several skills and rules which sailors call "seamanship." The new sailor must be taught how to bring a boat up to a mooring or alongside a landing, and to pilot the craft according to traffic regulations which, on the waterways, are known as the Rules of the Road. To be a good seaman, one must sail both safely and well; this makes the subjects of safety afloat (which includes some knowledge of the behavior of weather, particularly thunder squalls and fog) and of basic knots vitally important preparations to sailing.

A great deal of one's interest in sailing may depend upon selection of the right boat. One of the book's longer chapters is devoted to assisting the reader in weighing the numerous choices of new and second-hand boats, types and construction of hull, rig, sails, and yearly maintenance.

There is no ideal boat for every person and situation, so the choice must be something of a compromise. The new skipper must decide whether he wants a narrow, deep boat which will climb to windward in the fastest, liveliest fashion, but be quick in her motions when the winds and seas are rugged; or a beamy, shallower craft which slides fast off the wind and rides more comfortably in rougher seas.

If in this chapter and elsewhere the writer stresses some of the responsibilities and possible pitfalls involved in owning a boat, it must be strongly emphasized that the joys of sailing far outweigh all other aspects. Thousands upon thousands of men and women through the ages have known the thrills and exhilaration of handling the tiller of a smart craft, the joys of boat ownership, or the pleasure of sailing as crew.

Being a book primarily for the beginner, the writer has endeavored to make it simple. This is not always easy, for sailing is both a simple and a complex art. Sails have propelled craft for centuries. While there have been notable hull and sail refinements, their approximate shapes have remained essentially the same through the ages, and the increases in speed, it must be admitted, have been negligible in comparison with the accomplishments of mechanically propelled modes of travel by land, sea, and air. Nevertheless, sailing has always fascinated man, no more so than in this hurrying mid-20th century.

A small boat with a mast, a few stays, a sail or two, and a rope here and there, appears to be quite a simple mechanism. It can be properly so termed; but this simplicity also may be misleading, for sailing is a science, too. Physics and some scientific education are needed to design and rig a boat which will sail properly. The men who built Brooklyn Bridge and other early great bridges freely acknowledged a debt to Donald McKay and others for the stresses and strains they worked out in staying the spars that supported the clouds of canvas on the great clipper ships.

Yet, it was not until the development of heavier-than-air flying craft that a full realization was reached, by studies of the aerodynamics of sail, just how and why a boat reacted as she did to the forces of the wind. There is both art and science to sailing a boat, through the mastery of balance and control in a way to produce those few extra feet per mile which permits her to arrive at a destination ahead of a sister craft sailing in the same winds and waters.

As sailing is complex, the reader should bear in mind that while the book is a step-by-step guide in how to learn to sail, it is most important that it first be considered as a whole. Its proper use calls for the reader to read through all its fifteen chapters, then go back when starting to engage in practical sailing for a part-by-part reading on theory, rigging, handling on all points of sailing, and finally seamanship, from rules through weather to maintenance.

As a guide to how to sail for beginners, this book cannot pretend to say all one should know about this fascinating sport. Two of the more recent developments or refinements, dry sailing and planing, have been touched on only briefly. The former is certainly of considerable immediate interest to the beginner, and the latter provides the sailor with some of his greatest thrills. The planing boat is not for the novice any more than is racing, unless one is able to begin as a member of a class in junior or other group instruction.

Though the purpose is to teach sailing, not racing, the art of sailboat racing cannot be completely divorced from plain sailing, as frequent references herein will show. Sailboat racing deserves full and separate treatment. Nevertheless the writer would be remiss if he did not acknowledge, as must almost all writers about sailing, an indebtedness to the sport of yacht racing.

This guide to sailing has been made possible by the writer's long interest in junior and intercollegiate yacht racing. The thousands of youngsters in junior yachting—most particularly the members of Marblehead's famous Pleon Yacht Club—and their older brothers and sisters in intercollegiate yacht racing, whom the writer has known in the last 30-odd years, have in a very real sense contributed to this little volume.

To Walter C. "Jack" Wood, a wonderful teacher of the sport of sailing, who has also been a mentor of this writer, special thanks are due for his patient and helpful assistance on reading and correcting the numerous drafts which go into a book. Acknowledgment is also due Stephen Miles and Roger Stone for their assistance with the drawings; to Miss Gengean Keating, my secretary and an enthusiastic sailor, who has worked long and overtime on its preparation; and, not the least, to my severest critic, my wife, and all my family for their patience and understanding.

1. Sailing — It's the Life!

Sailing: can there be a grander sport? It is fun, it is thrilling, it is competitive, it is healthy, and it's marvelous therapy. Initiative, resourcefulness, and self-reliance are called forth by all phases.

The elements play a greater role in sailing than in any other sport. With sail and helm a skipper takes advantage of the wind and sea in order to maneuver and control his craft. This should be a cooperative venture, not a struggle against the elements, although occasionally man must battle wind and sea for survival.

Alfred Stanford, in his enchanting "The Pleasures of Sailing," rightly maintains, ". . . it is the boat that does the sailing. It is up to the man to catch on—to see and to feel the boat . . . it is the wind, not the man, that drives the boat. The man is the servant of the wind."

By learning to feel his craft a skipper may guide and control her, except in those rare instances when the rampages of nature become too forceful to cope with, as in hurricanes or severe squalls. The exhilaration which comes from using the wind to take you wherever you wish to go gives sailing its greatest of many appeals. Nothing is more stimulating than the feel of your hand upon a lively boat's tiller, with the wind blowing on your face as she sails saucily toward her destination.

Sailors have strong beliefs and strong feelings about their sport. The Arabians said, "Sailing is victory." Stanford and many others call sailing a way of life. Perhaps that is why, to sailors, there is always something distinctive, more appealing, about a family who sails.

Sailing is a great equalizer. There are times when brute force is helpful, even demanded; but the small man, the frail man, the crippled man, may all enjoy and even excel at sailing. Charlie Hoppin lost all strength in one arm as a result of polio—he couldn't even haul a sheet with this hand—yet, he became one of the truly great college dinghy skippers of the last decade, leading Harvard to two national championships.

The writer has known a number of veteran yachtsmen, unable to get about ashore without the aid of wheelchairs or crutches, who despite having to crawl about boats on hands and knees were excellent sailors and seamen, competing in

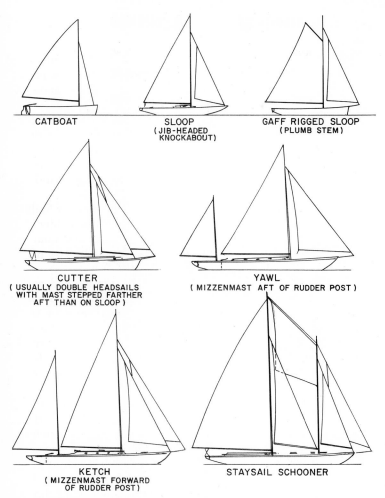

CATBOAT

SLOOP
(JIB-HEADED
KNOCKABOUT)

GAFF RIGGED SLOOP
(PLUMB STEM)

CUTTER
(USUALLY DOUBLE HEADSAILS
WITH MAST STEPPED FARTHER
AFT THAN ON SLOOP)

YAWL
(MIZZENMAST AFT OF RUDDER POST)

KETCH
(MIZZENMAST FORWARD
OF RUDDER POST)

STAYSAIL SCHOONER

Types of Sailboat Rigs. Every sailor should learn to recognize the rigs and characteristics of the more popular yacht types.

top-notch classes, or cruising and racing offshore. To them, as to Franklin Delano Roosevelt, sailing and cruising were therapy. At Marblehead's 1959 Race Week an outstanding performer was 16-year-old Daniel Mullane, a polio victim who three years earlier despaired of ever engaging in any of the competitive sports he loved.

Few sports offer greater equality of sexes. The fair sex can handle most jobs on small boats as well as, and sometimes better than, men or boys. A good sailor often acts instinctively, and here a woman's intuitiveness stands her in good stead. Attention to details is an attribute of crack skippers, and who could compare with a woman's love of attention to small detail? Lorna Whittelsey Hibbard, Frances McElwain Wakeman, Allegra Knapp Mertz, and a few others have been very close to

Left. **Sailing is a family sport! Mom, Dad, and kiddies haul out a 15′ Albacore, combination day-sailer and racer, for storage ashore on trailer between sails, called "dry sailing." Trailers are rolled into water for launching and hauling. (Courtesy, George D. O'Day Associates)** *Right:* **The whole family sails during a day at the beach by bringing a Sailfish, sailing surfboard type, in "over the road dry sailing" on the car top. (Courtesy, Alcort, Inc.)**

attaining first rank in helmsmanship—and who is to say a girl may not win the North American Junior Championship, defend the America's Cup, or win the Bermuda or Honolulu Race?

This is a book about sailing small boats. The term here will mean boats measuring under 30′ overall length. Small boats call for no apologies, for they make superb trainers of good sailors, provide great fun, and are thrilling to sail by anyone from 8 to 80. Charles H. W. Foster, an extremely inquisitive sailor who contributed much to the development of small boat yachting, commenced sailing in 1875 and was at the helm of his own boat only a few days before his death at 95.

If a person can sail a small boat, especially a small centerboard craft, he can sail any vessel. She will teach almost everything a sailor needs to know, but a big-boat skipper sometimes can be "lost" on a small yacht.

In this day and age we are often troubled by what Justice Louis D. Brandeis so aptly called "the curse of bigness." We must have the biggest TV screen, the biggest, showiest automobile, or the biggest business. One should not be led into such competition when acquiring a boat. Any boat represents something of a compromise, but one's choice should not be based on Mr. Jones' ownership of a 50-footer.

Whatever his choice of craft, to many a sailor she is a living being rather than an inanimate object. To her loving owner, an old hooker is a lovely lady. All sailors delight in admiring the sweet lines of a handsome craft. She is (in the Keats phrase), "A thing of beauty . . . a joy forever." A skipper's affection for a boat usually grows with time. This is why he possesses strong desires to maintain his fair lady, and why maintenance is sometimes called "ship's husbandry." A boy often treats his boat with the same affection as he does his dog.

Perhaps here is a good place to note that those who man small boats are skippers, helmsmen, yachtsmen, or sailors, but never, never, "boaters." One sails but never "skippers" a boat. A crew is any person on board a yacht, including at times the skipper.

A few have the mistaken idea that the word "yacht" connotes a plush craft of considerable size, where owners and guests in blue coats and white flannels are waited upon by flunkies, while hardy professionals do all the work of sailing. A conscious effort to avoid the words "yacht" and "yachtsmen" results. Nothing is farther from the truth, for the definition of "yacht" given by Webster and other authorities is: "any of various relatively small ships, vessels, or boats for pleasure cruises, racing and sailing." The yachtsman sails such a craft, and yachtsmanship is the practice or skill of maneuvering a yacht.

To become a good helmsman one must acquire the ability to sense where, why, and how his craft wants to go. Again quoting Alfred Stanford, "There must be a curiosity, a wonder in the heart of a good man at a vessel's helm." Such curiosity usually leads to understanding of boat, wind, and sea, whence a skipper acquires the "touch" that makes his craft dance to windward through the sea. There are born sailors—men who seem to have an intuitive sense of just the right thing to do at the right moment. Ray Hunt and Arthur Knapp are among many the writer has known. There are also "made" sailors. If one has any feel for sailing, one can acquire the skill to become a fine skipper by careful study and observation of wind, weather, water, hull, rigging, and sails.

The late Charles Francis Adams, Secretary of the Navy under President Hoover and the skipper who successfully defended the America's Cup with *Resolute* in 1920, was once posed this question in the writer's presence: "Mr. Adams, I suppose you know everything there is to know about sailing?" Turning upon the questioner that cold look for which his illus-

Left. **Finn Monotypes represent the acme of sailing single-handed. Sailing alone early in small catboat—as Johnny Marvin, 1956 bronze medalist in Olympics off Melbourne, handles this larger Finn—will perfect skills. (Courtesy, M.I.T. Nautical Assn.)** *Right.* **A master of downwind sailing engages in a type of single-handed sailing NOT recommended for novices. George O'Day, 1957 North American senior titlist, sails an International 14-footer—sportiest of small racing machines—handling tiller, mainsheet, spinnaker guy and sheet alone.**

Left. **Among the more popular small sailing cruisers is the 26′ Amphibi-Con, which, as her name implies, takes to the road as well as to water. "Chuck" Angle of Rochester, N. Y., 1958 champion, once used this "dry-sailing"** *Triangle II* **as a weekend trailer home while skiing at Stowe, Vt. (Courtesy, Mount Desert Yacht Yard, Inc.)** *Right.* **Planing, while not for beginners, is something to anticipate! Despite her short rig, a centerboard International 5-0-5 starts to lift out of water for a plane which gives far greater speed than normal at reaching for a 16½′ craft. Keel boats "surfboard" in seas but will not keep the sustained planes of planing hulls. (Courtesy, George D. O'Day Associates.)**

trious ancestors were famous, "Deacon" Adams replied scornfully, "Hell, no! I learn something every time I go sailing. If I didn't, it wouldn't be any fun!"

This same skipper, who had the ability to edge a boat to windward in a fashion his rivals described as "sideways," once spent two hours in the *Boston Globe* Sports Department studying a photograph of one of his racing boats, turning the picture this way and that and trying to find the answer to some little problem concerning sails that troubled him. Attention to detail!

Such study of sailing permits and leads to perfection, and the man who loves sailing is only too happy in this effort. It is part of the fun, and it pays the racing skipper tremendous dividends.

As a junior, George O'Day cherished the desire to win the

Sears Cup, emblematic of the North American Junior Championship; but the honor was denied him by, of all people, his best friend, Bobby Coulson. In analyzing his abilities later, George reached the conclusion there were some skippers who possessed the talent to sail a boat to windward just a tiny bit better than his own capabilities allowed. He decided the only way to achieve top rank as a helmsman called for perfecting other skills.

How well O'Day accomplished this goal was shown in 1957, when he won the Mallory Cup for the North American Senior Men's Championship. Not once in eight races did he lead all his seven rivals to the first or windward mark; yet, George's ability to sail a Thistle, a comparatively strange boat, off the wind, decided the issue. His craft overtook ten boats on reaches and runs, usually under spinnaker, to pick up the points needed to win the title from some of North America's very finest skippers.

Similar attention to detail, particularly the study of wind, weather, and tactics, made Bill Cox successively North American Junior Champion, titlist of Long Island Sound's famed International One-Designs, the nation's top team-racing authority, and twice champion of the International Lightning Class.

Keeping a happy ship is among the most important functions of a good skipper. On such a boat the helmsman supplements his knowledge with instinct. His decisions are confident, his hunches good, his crew is consulted, and he assigns each man to handle those functions of sailing for which he is best qualified.

A skipper must make decisions, for a boat cannot be run like a political convention. At the same time, no skipper should have inflated ideas of either his abilities or indispensabilities; for no man can know everything about rigging, sailmaking, carpentry, piloting, helmsmanship, meteorology, and half a dozen other skills needed in sailing a boat. An overfussy, or a screaming, cursing skipper spoils his own enjoyment and his crew's fun.

Some people just were not born to be good skippers. Yet, they can love and enjoy sailing—and make themselves as invaluable as the very best skipper. A crewman can have tremendous fun in perfecting his skills and learning to anticipate the moves of his skipper. Behind the best skipper usually is found at least one excellent crewman—and, very often, a splendid team.

When sailing dinghies and other small boats, a crew knowing when to hike, anticipate a tack, drop the centerboard prior to rounding a buoy, how to set a spinnaker without fuss, and to keep his skipper informed of the position of other boats, is worth his weight in gold. A good crew may suggest, but never tell, what decision to make; nor does he argue after one is made. Successful college dinghy skippers usually have a single crew of this sort through two, three, sometimes four years of competition.

No small part of Mike Vanderbilt's three successful defenses of the America's Cup stemmed from his happy ability to organize a crew and make use of the very best talents of each man. In the 1934 victory of *Rainbow* over *Enterprise,* after the American boat was two races down, it was Vanderbilt's willingness to submerge his personal role that turned the tide. He called upon Sherman Hoyt to handle *Rainbow* when under a genoa jib, a job at which Hoyt excelled, and borrowed Frank Paine from *Yankee* to set and trim the new parachute spinnakers.

Similar self-effacement in 1958 by Don Matthews in gathering a talented crew and calling upon Bus Mosbacher, a great small boat skipper, to start races and sail *Vim* to windward, made a "happy ship" and a dangerous contender. Anyone loving sailing can find his particular niche.

Aside from the fun, man gains respect for the sea. One has only to watch the breakers in a severe storm tear a sandy shore apart, or toss great blocks of granite from a wharf or breakwater, to understand its tremendous force and power, greater than any boat or man's. The Great Lakes can be as destructive as the oceans in this respect.

Self-reliance is perhaps the greatest lesson which sailing teaches. Juvenile delinquency is practically non-existent among youngsters who sail boats. Sailing is a way of life in which men or women match their abilities against the elements in an untamed, primitive world, much as their ancestors battled the wilderness. The plain, oft-quoted virtues of pioneer America play a part in sailing well—courage, determination, foresight, self-reliance, neatness, discipline, and diligence. A man who sails usually loves life and is apt to possess humor, strength, and wisdom.

Moreover, small boat sailors are in a sense a fraternity within the larger brotherhood of the sea. There is the companionship which grows between skipper and crew, in fact even exists between skipper and boat. In the broader sense, there are the tremendous friendships which sailing engenders. Many a young man or woman has found sailing the key to a whole new outlook on life, or to new friendships when transferred from their home environment.

Last, but not least, there is the pure joy and fun of sailing. On first thought the new yachtsman may wonder, "What has cruising to do with me and my small craft?" Cruising is discovery, exploring. There may be an island just offshore or in the middle of the lake that you have longed to explore, which a boat now makes possible. Whether on sea, lake, or river, there is always the anticipation of what lies beyond the next point—the place just over the horizon. The cove or harbor, only two or three miles down the shore, looks entirely different when viewed from a boat.

While not immediately for the beginner, there is the joy of moonlight sailing as the path of pale light sparkles across the water, giving a wonderful, lustrous, soft outline to even the most rugged shore. The challenges of night sailing without a moon, and of thick weather, give to skipper and crew a wonderful exhilaration when the objective is attained.

Later, in larger boats, a landfall—first a pinpoint, then a slim lighthouse on the horizon, and finally the emerging land—provides a real thrill. Not to be overlooked is the fun of postmortems, talking over a race sailed or cruises made with other sailors. Even the chores of looking after a boat become part of the pleasure of sailing.

Every sailor feels a happier, healthier man or woman for having been afloat, whether guiding his craft through whimsical airs or rail breezes. What sailor has not thrilled to the feel of his boat beating to windward on a bright day when brisk northwest winds turn the sea into a field of blown cotton? What pure content, sailing home at sunset! Skipper and crew are at peace with the world after a perfect day afloat when sense of time has almost been lost.

Before going into the infinite but joyful details of learning to sail small boats, let us remember what the Water Rat said in Kenneth Grahame's *The Wind in the Willows:* "Believe me, my young friend, there is *nothing*—half so much worth doing as simply messing about in boats. Simply messing ... messing—about—in—boats; messing—. . . about in boats—or *with* boats . . . In or out of 'em, it doesn't matter. Nothing seems really to matter, that's the charm of it. Whether you get away, or whether you don't; whether you arrive at your destination or whether you reach somewhere else, or whether you never get anywhere at all, you're always busy, and you never do anything in particular; and when you've done it there's always something else to do . . ."

When it comes to messing around in boats, nothing is better than a sailboat.

2. Nomenclature and Basic Parts of a Sailboat

Before beginning to sail, one should acquire a knowledge of the basic parts of a sailboat—hull, spars, rigging, and sails. This knowledge should cover both the nomenclature and functions of each part.

There are those who will pooh-pooh, or profess to be mystified by, nautical terms. Yet, every sport has, to a certain extent, its own language and phraseology. Are "tack" and "jibe," "port," or "starboard" any more obscure or baffling to the uninitiated than such words as "slalom" and "sitzmark" from skiing, or "eagle" and "birdie" in golf? "Ready about—Hard-a-lee!" is a warning of exactly the same nature as the golfer's cry, "Fore!"

Nautical terminology is an honored language with an older tradition than the phraseology of any other sport, and worthy of cultivation. As one learns about boats, an understanding will develop as to the sources from which many nautical words stem.

Without delving deeply into this subject, a good example is the word "starboard." Ancient double-ended Norse ships were steered by a sort of rudder fastened to the right side of the vessel just forward of the stern. Thus, the right side of a Viking ship came to be known as the "steer-board" side—a term later corrupted to "starboard." The left side, now called "port," was once "larboard," possibly from "laden," as cargo was loaded here.

The first step toward becoming a sailor is to examine a boat in detail to learn her basic parts. One will note that, in English, it is customary to speak of ships and boats as if they were women. As Kipling wrote, ". . . the liner, she's a lady." Even when boats are named for men—a custom rare in yachts and pleasure craft, but common in commercial ships—a boat is always referred to as "she" or "her," NEVER "it."

The Hull

The forward part of a boat is always called the **bow**, rather than the front. When walking toward the bow, one goes "forward," not "up front." The bow, the general term for the forward part, is also used to designate the foremost portion of a craft. The extreme bow of a boat is better referred to as the **stem,** a structural member of the vessel usually made of a hard wood such as oak. It is permissible, however, when commenting on the appearance of a boat, to say "She has a pretty bow," even though referring to the curve of the stem. Modern small sailboats usually have a straight or plumb bow, a short curved overhang known as a spoon bow, or a modification of these types.

Looking forward toward the bow, the **right** side is the **starboard** and the **left** is **port.** In giving steering directions, our Navy now uses left and right for port and starboard, though amateur sailors still prefer the traditional usage.

Turn and look in the opposite direction. One is now facing **aft,** not looking "back," or "to the rear." The word is aft, not after, although the latter is permitted in combination with other words, such as after-body and after-guard. The aft end of a craft is known as the **stern.** In small sailboats a **transom** stern, which is broad and usually slightly inclined forward from the deck toward the water, is the most common. Keel boats tend to have overhanging sterns or counters, which add a graceful look, and a few craft have canoe sterns almost identical to their bows.

If the boat is decked, the open portion where the skipper steers and the crew sits is known as the **cockpit.** The portion under the deck, near the mast, is often referred to as the **cuddy.** In larger boats, this space extending aft to the cockpit is devoted to a cabin, which grows more spacious as the craft increases in size. Cruising sailboats have cabins divided into several parts—the main cabin, galley, staterooms, forecastle (crew's quarters), etc.

Cockpits may be made watertight and self-bailing, but small boats usually have open cockpits with floorboards covering the inside of the hull (bilge). A seat running across the boat is usually referred to as an amidships **thwart.** If there is a deck aft, the space enclosed like a closet is called the **lazarette.** The center of the boat, where cabin and cockpit are found, is known as **amidships.** The extreme width of the boat, which occurs amidships, is known as the **beam.** Land or vessels seen from a boat are spoken of as lying abeam (if at right angles) or forward or aft (sometimes abaft) the beam.

The **skipper,** a term synonymous with helmsman in small boats, steers or maneuvers his craft by means of a **rudder** actuated by a **tiller** or **steering wheel.** Small boats rarely have steering wheels, a device which eases the labor of steering by means of a gear between the wheel and the rudder post. A tiller is connected directly with the rudder or rudder post. Weather and sea conditions are rarely so severe as to prevent a person from steering his sailboat by this direct method. Steering with a tiller (**helm**) increases the ability of a helmsman to feel the reaction of his boat to wind and sea.

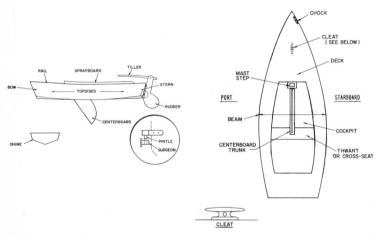

Left. Profile of small centerboard sailboat with inserts illustrating rudder fittings and chine. **Right.** Birdseye view of small sailboat hull and deck. Insert shows cleat.

A sailboat is kept upright by the shape of the underbody (that portion of the hull normally submerged), which creates forces to oppose those made by the pressure of wind on sails and rigging. This factor, called stability, is designed into the hull. Centerboards and keels are a major, though not entire, means of effecting such stability.

A centerboard boat may be likened to a slab of wood. When lying flat in the water, it possesses a great deal of stability because the centers of gravity and buoyancy act together. If the plank is slowly tilted until it is nearly on edge, the forces no longer tend to act to right the boat. Thus a centerboard craft, when severely **heeled** (tipped), has its least stability, i.e., ability to stay upright.

A keel craft may be better compared to a log in the water, as its underwater sections often are comparatively round. A log will spin when any force is applied above the water. If a fin, that is a strip of metal with a weight, is affixed, the log immediately gains stability, with the fin or keel acting as a counterbalance to any pressure applied above water.

A **keel** is built as a permanent part of the hull, and usually consists of a piece of oak to which a lead or iron weight is bolted at the bottom. The rudder normally is attached to the keel by means of a rudder post on its aft side running up into the hull to the cockpit, where the tiller or wheel is connected. The boat is steered by turning the rudder, not the tiller, in the direction toward which it is desired to maneuver the craft. The opposite is true with most geared steering wheels, for here the wheel and the rudder turn in the same direction.

A **centerboard,** which is found in most modern small boats, may be raised or lowered through a slot in the bottom of the boat. When not in use it is housed in a casing, known as the **centerboard trunk,** which protrudes into the cockpit or cabin. Centerboards may be made of metal, but today are usually constructed of wood or plastic, and very few now contain lead or iron weights. Most centerboards are pivoted. When boards may only be lowered or lifted vertically, they are known as daggerboards. Some very flat boats, notably scows raced on the inland lakes of the Midwest and Barnegat Bay, have two boards, one on each side of the hull. These are known as **lee or bilge boards.** The leeward board does most of the work as it is located in the bilge and inclined so as to be vertical when the boat heels to its usual sailing angle of about 15°.

Centerboards may be adjusted upward and downward to control the speed of a boat and the balance of the helm. They also permit operation in shallower waters than would be possible with deep keel craft.

Centerboard boats most frequently have their rudders placed at the end of a **skeg,** a piece of wood extending down and toward the stern from the center line of the underbody. If the rudder is attached to the transom, and partially out of water, it is referred to as an outboard, or "barn door," rudder.

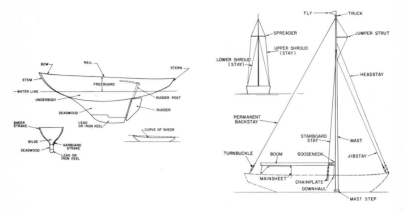

Left. Profile of a small keel sailboat with inserts showing sheer and cross-section of boat. Right. Rigging of small sailboat with profile insert of mast staying.

This type of rudder is used extensively on dinghies and other small boats; it has the very great advantage of permitting the novice to see, rather than visualize, the actions of helm and rudder in maneuvering a boat. Often it is also detachable, making for easy storage.

Pivoted rudders, where the rudder blade will pivot up if it strikes a submerged object or the bottom, are advantageous in shallow water; and balanced rudders, where a small portion of the area of the blade extends forward of the rudder post, are also used extensively.

The sides of a boat above the **waterline** are called **topsides,** and the piece of wood or plastic running fore and aft where the topsides meet the deck is known as the **rail,** while the distance from the waterline to the deck is termed **freeboard.** The curve of a boat's profile between bow and stern is referred to as her **sheer.**

The introduction of plastics is doing away with many traditional items of boat construction, but the sailor should know that wooden boats are built of planking over **frames** and **ribs,** usually oak, with pieces of wood known as **knees** strengthening decks and flooring at the joints. In a planked boat, a single plank is known as a **strake.** Thus the topmost plank is called the **sheer strake,** and the plank next to the keel or **deadwood** (solid timber above keel) is termed the **garboard strake.**

The turn or curve of the hull below the waterline is called the **bilge,** and one speaks of craft as being hard, flat, round, and soft-bilged, depending upon their underwater shape. The term bilge also is used for the lowest interior part of the hull where bilge water collects.

The Rig

The rigging of a sailboat falls into three basic categories: spars, standing and running rigging. The general term **spar** embraces any mast, boom, gaff, or yard used on sailing vessels.

All sailing craft carry their sails attached in some fashion to a **mast,** although **booms, gaffs, stays,** and **halyards** (also spelled **halliards**) play a role. Technically, every sailboat has a mainmast, but the prefix main is important only when a craft has more than one mast. Although sailing vessels have been built with as many as seven masts, the only masts other than mainmast one need know here are the **foremast** (or forward mast) on a two-masted schooner, and the **mizzenmast** or **jigger,** near the stern of a yawl or ketch. These can be identified in the diagrams on page 7. In small boats, our concern is only with the mainmast, hereinafter called the mast.

The mast is supported by stays. Those at the side of the mast are referred to as **sidestays,** or **shrouds.** They are attached by means of turnbuckles or rope to metal **chainplates** on, or built into, the hull. The stay leading to the bow is known as the **headstay.** Some boats also have additional stays, called jib and fore stays, leading forward from the mast.

Stays running aft are termed **backstays.** One attached from the head of the mast to the stern of the boat is named the permanent backstay. Some craft have **running backstays,** which lead from the mast, at the point of attachment to the jibstay, to either side of the deck, approximately midway from the mast to the stern. As their name implies, running backstays, unlike shrouds, are movable, and must be set up or cast off by means of tackles, slides, or levers whenever the boat is tacked. The backstay on the windward side is kept taut and the one to leeward loose or slack. Some boats rely entirely on a permanent backstay, which makes for a simplified rig.

When two sidestays are used to support a mast, a pair of

wooden or metal struts are attached to the mast at the junction point where the lower of the two stays from each side fastens to the spar. The upper sidestays lead over the ends of these struts, called **spreaders,** and then to the mast at a more effective angle to provide the necessary support. Larger, more complicated boats sometimes use a double set of spreaders.

Struts, either single or a fork-shaped pair on the forward side of the mast, placed above the jibstay are known as **jumper struts.** They carry jumper stays to assist the support of the spar.

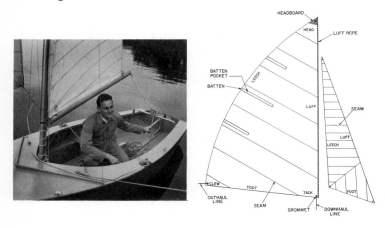

Left. **Ralph Evans of M.I.T., Silver Medal winner at 1948 Olympics, in cockpit of Firefly Dinghy rigged for single-handed sailing. Note jibsheets, cleats behind sprayboard, sidestays leading through deck, fairleads, cam-type jam cleats, and mainsheet rigged on a special traveller.** *Right.* **Diagram of mainsail and jib, designating principal parts.**

The main boom is attached to the mast by a universal joint known as a **gooseneck.** The lower part (foot) of a mainsail is attached to the boom. The in and out movement of the boom is controlled by a rope known as the **mainsheet.** It travels through a series of **blocks** (pulleys) on both boom and hull to assist the trimming of sails. One block is often attached to a rope or metal **traveller** at the stern to aid in bringing the mainsail to the proper angle in relation to the center of the boat for sailing to windward.

The mainsail is hoisted on the mast by means of a **halyard,** a rope running from the head of the sail up through a **sheave** (a wheel usually built into the top of the spar) and back to the deck where it is fastened to a cleat—usually, but not always, passing first through a block.

The jib is attached, usually by means of snaphooks, to the jibstay prior to being hoisted by halyard through a block on the forward side of the mast. Jibs ordinarily are trimmed by a pair of jibsheets running from the aft corner (clew) along the side of the boat to cleats, near or inside the cockpit. Some boats use a jib boom and traveller, whereby the jibsheet runs from the end of the boom to the traveller and forward to the jibstay before being led aft. This self-tending rig is a help to single-handed sailing. Both sheets and halyards are frequently made taut by the means of **winches,** geared drum mechanisms which permit proper hoisting and trimming with greater ease and efficiency than would otherwise be possible.

On each side of the bow near the stem is a metal fitting known as **chock,** through which anchor rodes, mooring lines, or painters may be led. A **painter** is the name used for the rope by which a small boat is attached to a float or pier, while a **rode** is synonymous with any rope or line attached to the anchor of such craft.

The Sail

The sail is the "engine" which harnesses the wind to drive a sailboat through the water.

The **mainsail** on most small boats is triangular, as are nearly all working sails—jibs, staysails, foresails, and mizzens—carried on modern boats. The **gaff rig,** with a four-sided mainsail, is still seen on a few older craft, frequently as a foresail on schooners, but it is becoming increasingly rare. The gaff mainsail and the fisherman staysail, also used on schooners, are the only exceptions to the rule of triangular working sails. As gaff sails on small sloops and catboats are nearly obsolete, the main concern here will be with triangular sails.

The three sides of such sails are known as the luff, leech, and foot. (See page 22.)

The **luff** is always the first part of any sail to enter the wind, and is called the leading edge. In a mainsail, the luff is hoisted along the mast on a track by means of slides sewn to the sail or by a luff rope in a grooved slot. The luff of a jib usually is hoisted along a stay. This luff is the edge that first meets the wind, and hence is the sail's most important part, for the area along the luff provides a major share of the driving power in any sail.

The **foot** is the portion of the mainsail lying along the boom between the **tack,** always the adjustable corner of a sail where the luff meets the foot, and the **clew,** the lower aft corner. The tack is attached to the gooseneck by a shackle or similar device led through a metal eye at the tack, known as a **cringle.**

The clew is usually made fast to an **outhaul** fitting near the end of the boom. This fitting often runs on a track, although on some small boats it may be only a piece of **line** (rope) led through an eye and made fast to a cleat on the boom. The fore and aft curve (**draft**) of a sail, a very important factor in

Left. **Rhodes 19-footer showing a good example of mast staying, including permanent backstay, shrouds, spreader, and jumper strut. Note cuddy forward of cockpit, mainsheet, traveller, and outboard rudder with tiller. (Courtesy, George D. O'Day Associates.)** *Right.* **A Blue Jay, one of the nation's most popular small boats for young sailors, showing the principal parts of a sail, including seams, reinforcing at corners, batten pockets, and mainsail attached to the boom by a track. (Courtesy, McKean Boats.)**

making a boat sail properly, is controlled by a combination of the tautness of halyard and outhaul, aided by a boom downhaul at the gooseneck.

The majority of sailboats attach the foot of the sail to the boom by means of track and slides, or a grooved spar. Most dinghies and some other small boats have loose-footed mainsails, which have the advantage of simplicity, as well as permitting a sail to take its proper curve naturally.

The **leech** is the third side—the edge from which the wind leaves the sail. Particularly on mainsails, this is not a straight line between the clew and the **head** or top of the sail. This curve, known as the **roach,** can be a very important factor in racing sails. To prevent a tendency of this longest edge to curl, **battens** may be used. Usually made of wood, although plastics or other materials are sometimes used, battens are narrow strips which fit into **batten pockets** sewn into the sail. Their primary purpose is to keep the leech from curling inward or falling off in a pronounced fashion. Battens of extreme length have been used to accentuate a sail's roach.

The halyard is attached to the head of the sail by means of a wooden or metal support known as the **headboard.** This distributes the strain, holds up the sail, and may be either separately attached or sewn into the sail. A hole in the headboard permits the halyard to be fastened by means of a shackle, snaphook, or knot.

It will be noted that sails are not a single piece of cloth but rather a series of strips sewn together. Sails have evolved through the years from woven mats of reeds through flax, canvas, and cotton duck to synthetic fabrics. Since the end of World War II, synthetics have virtually replaced cotton sails. Their great advantages stem from the fact that they do not shrink when wet nor deteriorate as fast under hard usage. Moreover, they tend to maintain their normal shape even after being severely strained in hard winds. Cotton sails stretch out of shape easily to lose their effectiveness and deteriorate from mildew.

The development of synthetic sails has been extremely rapid and new types of sails from those described here may be in vogue tomorrow. Most new sails for both large and small boats today are made of Dacron, woven polyester fibers. An exception occurs with spinnakers, which are generally made from nylon. Nylon was the first of the widely used synthetics, but one, unlike its successors, which proved prone to excessive stretching. Its preferred use in spinnakers stems from the fact that it is light, strong, and closely woven. Dacron is not as dense, and if woven as tightly as nylon it would be too heavy for spinnaker use. In other sails nylon was first replaced by Orlon, which has now given way to Dacron.

While sailcloths are generally sewn, there have been experiments with other methods of piecing sails together. One resulted in the use of a tape, rather than stitching, to adhere the luff rope to a sail. Transparent material has been used to put windows in sails, permitting the helmsman a better view to leeward, and a few completely transparent sails have been made for small boats.

The principal discussion here has been about mainsails. As noted, the jib (the triangular sail forward of the mast) has a luff, usually made with a wire luff rope, hoisted along a stay. The leech runs from the head to the clew in a line roughly parallel to the mast, although large overlapping jibs have a leech more nearly parallel to the leech of the accompanying mainsail. The foot of the jib runs from the tack to the clew, just above the deck. The tack is normally shackled to a deck fitting, although sometimes a downhaul is used. Jibsheets are attached to the clew by means of a snap shackle, snaphook, spliced rope or wire. A self-tending jib on a traveller may have a jib boom running the full or partial length of the foot.

The mainsail and the jib are controlled by ropes designated as the mainsheet or jibsheet. Note carefully that *the sheet is always a line or rope*, NEVER, strange as it may seem to the uninitiated, a piece of sailcloth. The surest way to spot a landlubber is to hear him refer to a sail as the sheet. Usually, sheets run through a set of pulleys, nautically called **blocks,** on the boom, deck, or hull, and are then fastened to cleats. Sometimes on the way they pass through eyes on the deck called **fairleads.** If a sail is large, a cylindrical winch often is used to assist the crew in hoisting and trimming sail. The winch is placed in a position between the blocks and the cleat, usually nearer the latter.

All modern sailboats carry a **jib-headed rig.** Many refer to this as a Marconi rig, which is really a misnomer. In the early days of this rig, an adaptation of earlier Bermudian and leg of mutton rigs, the spars were very tall and often curved at the top to aid the fit of racing sails. This required multiple staying and the resulting complexity of rigging resembled Marconi wireless masts, which had come into vogue a few years earlier. Hence such sailboat spars were called **Marconi masts.** Through careless usage, the term Marconi has been widely, but incorrectly, applied to the rig, as well as to the mast.

The name jib-headed rig derives from the fact the new mainsails, used on Marconi masts, were shaped and had a head resembling a jib—a sail in use for centuries. Thus a modern sailboat, even if only a catboat with a single (main) sail, is jib-head rigged.

3. The Points of Sailing

Before rigging a boat for the first sail, one should know the basic theory of what makes a sailboat go and the various points of sailing in relation to course and wind direction.

Even though man was doubtless making use of sail before starting to record his thoughts and history, there was no full understanding of what caused a sail to drive a boat through the water until quite recently. The first sailboats appear to have been river craft of the raft type on which a square or triangular sail, probably made of hides or woven reeds, was hung from a pole. As this accelerated the raft's downstream progress, early sailors assumed the wind's pressure on a sail was the sole driving force.

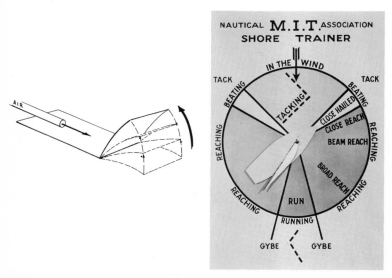

Left. Diagram of a simple experiment by which Dr. Manfred Curry illustrates the suction effect of the lee side of a mainsail when wind blows against windward side. Take a sheet of letter paper (not too light) and cut about 5″ long and 2–3″ wide. Bend one end to curve like a sail with v's of ½″ to ¾″ cut in sides at the bend. Place the lips at the opposite end of the paper and blow across top side. Notice how the "sail" lifts toward the blower rather than being pushed away by wind pressure. *Right.* The Shore Trainer, developed by Jack Wood for the Massachusetts Institute of Technology Nautical Association. (Courtesy, M.I.T.)

So long as boats sailed mainly or nearly before the wind, this assumption was not entirely mistaken. Yet, when man learned to sail across the wind—and later to tack to windward against the breeze—he continued to believe for ages that the wind blowing against his sail pushed his boat through the water. This belief persisted long after square sails were replaced on yachts by the fore-and-aft rig, which proved more efficient when sailing to windward by a series of right angle maneuvers called **tacks.**

Boats of Comet Class criss-cross while sailing (beating or tacking) to windward. (Morris Rosenfeld photo.)

Twentieth-Century experience with airplanes revolutionized this thinking, and the theory of aerodynamics of sails was born. During the decade after the Wright brothers first flew at Kitty Hawk, many believed air pressure on the underside of wings kept planes aloft. Only when the covering was ripped from top surfaces of wings was the importance of suction (lift) on the top of the wing generally realized.

Following this interesting discovery, experiments were made with boats and sails in the early 1920s on the Charles River

Basin, in laboratories and wind tunnels at Massachusetts Institute of Technology, and by Dr. Manfred Curry, an American living in Germany.

Data compiled, exchanged, and later published by Curry in his "Yacht Racing—The Aerodynamics of Sails" focused attention on the fact that when a boat was sailing to windward, or reaching relatively close-hauled, the side of the mainsail away from the wind (**leeward**) was a major factor in driving the boat, just as the upper side of an airplane wing provides lift.

A simple experiment, devised by Dr. Curry, graphically shows this point in an accompanying diagram. When a person blows across the top of a piece of paper, with one end fashioned to resemble a sail, this sail-like portion is drawn upward and toward the wind rather than being blown down and away.

Smoke bombs helped show that the wind's action in sweeping by the lee side of a mainsail created a suction effect which pulled the boat ahead. It was also discovered that by increasing the size of the jib and creating a sizeable slot between the leeward side of the mainsail and the windward side of the jib, boats sailed considerably faster. This led to the use of large, overlapping genoa jibs on racing boats.

From this brief description of the aerodynamics involved in sailing, the next step is a discussion of the various points of sailing: reaching, running, and beating (sailing to windward).

Walter C. "Jack" Wood, Director of Sailing at M.I.T. since 1935, has probably taught more people to sail than any man in the United States. In the course of these years, he has come to believe the points of sailing can be best visualized through the use of circles. One method is a board with a circle divided into colored sectors, which illustrates graphically the various points of sailing. Another circle, with a series of boats on its circumference, diagrams the relation of wind to the sails. As a boat "sails" the complete circle, she engages in all points of sailing and makes the principal maneuvers needed to sail a boat.

Examine first the M.I.T. Nautical Association Shore Trainer. Shadings and words show the sectors of the circle on the board.

A large quadrant of 90° will be noted in the upper sector of the circle. This area of 45° on each side of the wind direction (represented by 0° or 360°) is one in which a craft cannot trim her sails sufficiently flat to sail. If she heads higher toward

the wind, her sails start luffing and flapping. She is then said to be **"in the wind."** Some boats sail closer to the wind than others, but even the most close-winded craft seldom achieves better than 40° (3½ points) to the wind. One compass poi\t is 11¼°.

This leaves a narrow area or sector, approximating 45° from the wind's direction, in which a vessel's course is described as **close hauled.** This is the white sector on the M.I.T. Trainer. The sailor's term for this type of sailing is **beating to windward.** Another way of expressing it is to say a craft is **laying** or sailing as close to the wind as she can sail with advantage; for when she points too high and her sails flap, the speed drops. This point of sailing takes more skill on the part of the helmsman than any other and will be discussed in detail in a special chapter.

Suffice to say here that in order to reach a point which lies within 45° of the direction from which the wind is blowing, a boat must beat or tack to windward on a zigzag course, with

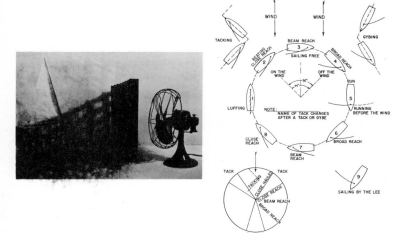

Left. **M.I.T. Shore Trainer adapted for a practical demonstration with a free-swinging and pivoted model boat superimposed on the Trainer's board. Electric fan simulates actual wind through an intervening grid. Note man's hand, at left, trimming sail. (Courtesy, M.I.T.)** *Right.* **Circular diagram for teaching points of sailing and maneuvers, designed by Jack Wood for use at M.I.T. Note: A boat, moving clockwise from position 1 fully around the circle to position 2 again engages in all points of sailing and principal maneuvers.**

a series of 90° changes of direction, or tacks, until the objective is attained (see dotted lines in top sector of illustration, M.I.T. Trainer).

Looking at the very bottom of the trainer's circle, a sector slightly larger than the close-hauled section and labeled **run** will be found. Here a boat has the wind blowing from a direction opposite to that in which she is headed and the craft is said to be on a **run,** or **running before the wind.** A boat's course here is within one or two compass points of 180° opposite to the wind's direction. When running, yachts usually have their booms as far forward as the shrouds will permit, and, when racing, normally carry a spinnaker on the opposite side. Sloops often have their jibs winged out on the windward side.

The areas of the circle which fall between the beating and running sectors are designated by the broad term, **reaching.**

Reaching falls into three classifications known as **close, beam,** and **broad reaching,** which are labelled on the trainer, although without pie-shaped sections. The difference between **close reaching** and sailing to windward is small. Here, instead of sailing as close to the wind as possible with advantage, a boat heads for a fixed point (sailing on course). The wind is generally coming from forward of abeam (amidships) and sheets may be eased (slacked) slightly to increase speed.

When a boat's course is approximately at right angles to the wind, she is **beam reaching.** Her course is to a fixed point and sheets have been eased off more than when close reaching.

The fairly large area between beam reaching and running is described as **broad reaching.** Here the sails are slacked off considerably, the angle depending upon how far aft the wind is blowing, and it is often possible to add light sails, such as spinnakers, to increase speed.

Though the impression is often to the contrary, sailboats are not traveling fastest when the wind is astern. Actually, a boat attains her greatest speed when sailing a full-and-bye course just off the wind on the thin edge dividing windward sailing from close reaching. In many boats, it is more advantageous to zig-zag down the breeze, with a series of jibes and broad reaches, than to run dead to leeward. This is known as **jibing** or **tacking to leeward.**

The M.I.T. Shore Trainer can have a model boat mounted on a free-swinging and pivoting stand at the center of the colored circle. Then, by placing an electric fan and an intervening grid in front of the trainer to simulate actual wind, a boat may be put through her paces of beating, reaching, running, tacking, and jibing.

Another means of illustrating the points of sailing is the circular diagram with 8 boats sketched on its circumference. Here, a boat starts in the wind as though leaving a mooring or float (Pos. 1). She falls off to close-hauled on port tack, then progresses around the circle to beam reaching, broad reaching, running, jibing (changing) to starboard tack, broad reaching, beam reaching, close reaching and finally tacking back to port once more (Pos. 1 & 2). The fine points of sailing by the lee, jibing, tacking, luffing, and sailing free or off the wind also are indicated on this fine trainer. Both diagrams should be of assistance when reading subsequent chapters.

4. Bending Sail — Leaving Mooring or Float

It is assumed the beginner has read through this book before attempting practical sailing so that, in addition to being introduced to the parts of a boat, the theory and points of sailing, he has acquired a least an elementary knowledge of knots, safety, and rules of the road; these will be needed in preparing for and taking the first sail.

It is advisable to have an experienced person, if available, help the new sailor put into practice what he has read and

Left. Charley Shumway, top dinghy skipper, and his wife, instruct a potential girls' champion of 1970 in rigging a Sprite prior to launching from trailer. Can you identify headstay, sail track, headboard, gooseneck, mast step, thwart, centerboard trunk, mainsheet, tiller, traveller, rudder, and gudgeon? (Courtesy, George D. O'Day Associates.) *Right.* Preparing for a college regatta, at the U. S. Naval Academy, the crew of a Tempest leads sail luff into slot of a grooved spar prior to hoisting. (Courtesy, U. S. Navy.)

accompany the novice until he gains enough experience to have confidence in his own ability to handle a boat.

Upon boarding his boat, a skipper notes first if there is water in the bilge, then checks whether anything is amiss with running and standing rigging. A frayed rope, bent shackle, unscrewed turnbuckle or a cleat worked loose from the deck might spell trouble. First, the craft should be pumped and

Details of sail hoisting. At left, crew sways up on halyard led around mast cleat; at right, fair crew assists skipper in making the boom downhaul taut.

sponged dry, for water sloshing in the bilge is the wrong kind of **ballast** (weight added to hull). If you live where showers and storms are frequent, a canvas or plastic cover to keep rain from the open cockpit is a good investment, saving hours of bailing.

Assuming all gear is shipshape, the next job is bending on the mainsail. If the sail is properly stowed, the head is on top and can be led from the bag without dumping the whole sail on deck.

The headboard is first attached to the halyard. A wire halyard will likely have a **shackle** (U-shaped securing device with pin). Rope halyards require tying a knot through the headboard, although some will be spliced to a snaphook. If a knot is required, two half hitches, or preferably the buntline hitch (minor variations are called topsail sheet or studdingsail tack bends), are recommended. Some prefer to put the sail onto the mast before attaching the halyard; it matters little, but don't forget to tie the halyard temporarily to some object to avoid losing it up the mast.

With the halyard secured, the luff rope is fed into a groove or, via slides, onto a track on the mast. A well-equipped boat will have a stopper or lock to hold the sail until ready to hoist. The tack is now secured to the gooseneck shackle and the foot

35

removed from the sailbag to permit the clew to be led to the outhaul, feeding sail to boom groove or track simultaneously.

When the sail has been attached to the outhaul fitting and pulled taut, it is a good moment to ship a rudder of the detachable outboard type. Some rudders fit on a heavy track, similar to those used on masts, while others attach by slipping two pins, called **pintles,** on the rudder into **gudgeons** (fittings with eyes) bolted to the stern. Some may prefer to ship the rudder before bending any sail. Next, affix a tiller, if detachable, to the rudder.

Going forward, the skipper should slack his mainsheet off the cleat and shake loose the coil so the sail may be hoisted with the boom free of any lashings. Next, free any inboard tiller if it's tied in one position and lower the boat's centerboard.

The mainsail may be hoisted now or after jib has been bent on but NOT HOISTED. The mainsail should be hauled up ("two-blocked," as sailors say) until the headboard shackle reaches the masthead sheave. This may require using a winch or swaying on the halyard. The boom down-haul helps make a luff taut. In cleating the halyard, that is in passing the rope in crisscross fashion over the cleat, it is recommended the final loop be a slip hitch (a small **bight,** or loop, slipped back under the rope just before the last turn) rather than a half hitch which can jam and takes time to shake loose.

When boats are at floats, leave hoisting any sail until just prior to casting off, particularly if other boats are tied up. This will prevent bumping hulls.

Bending a jib is a similar operation to bending on mainsail. To prevent loose sail from slipping overboard, the tack should be attached to the jibstay fitting first, then snaphooks bent to the stay with the sail held between the arms and finally the halyard shackle attached. Now, when required, attach the jib sheets. If jib is bent on early, place a sail stop around the loose canvas until ready to hoist.

The craft should now be ready to cast off her painter or mooring lines. An experienced hand, if available, should take the tiller and give practical demonstrations on how to handle the boat before turning the helm over to a new sailor. Regardless of the presence of the recommended instructor, the beginner should have a knowledge of how to handle the craft before attempting to get under way. The absence of an experienced sailor means the novice must exercise special caution.

The first sail will probably start from a mooring or float. The latter is somewhat easier from which to operate when not crowded with other boats. When starting the sail from a wharf try to have your boat tied with its bow headed into the wind, or at least with the wind coming from some point abeam or forward thereof. Only the experienced sailor should attempt to leave a float when the breeze is blowing his boat directly against the pier, for this represents essentially what

Dinghies leaving float of M.I.T. Sailing Pavilion. Flag on building indicates dinghies are headed into the wind. However, No. 23 and the unrigged dinghy alongside are in best position; they lay head-to-wind without bumping dock and can depart easily on a beam reach. (Courtesy, M.I.T.)

everyone who has read sea stories knows as a **lee shore**, to be avoided as a difficult spot from which to maneuver a sailboat.

Assuming the craft is tied, head to wind, with sails hoisted and a crew of two aboard, the skipper takes his place at the helm in a position permitting completely free movement of the tiller to either side of the boat. The crew stands on the float holding the painter or headstay.

The skipper makes his choice as to the best tack for leaving the float. If he selects **starboard tack**—that is, with the wind coming over the boat's starboard rail and boom out to port—the helmsman sits to starboard with tiller in left hand and mainsheet in right.

At the command "Cast off!" his crew unties the painter, grasps forestay in right hand, and pushes the boat's starboard side, usually with his foot, away from the float as he leaps onto the bow. In dinghy types lacking a foredeck, the crew is more apt to hold the sidestay, place his left foot inside the boat aft of the shrouds, and shove off with his right foot and/or hand.

When calling "Cast off!" the skipper pulls tiller toward his boat's starboard side and gradually hauls in his sail until it fills and the boat gathers way.

When the first sail starts from a mooring, the maneuver is quite similar. The helmsman takes a position which will place him on the windward side when the sails fill. His crew goes forward, uncleats the mooring line, or buoyed anchor rode, slips it from the chock, and at the command "Cast off!" pulls the mooring rope smartly aft in order to give the boat some steerageway before tossing the marking buoy into the water.

The skipper pulls his helm up (toward the windward side) and allows the boat to pay off. The maneuver may be expedited in a sloop by having the crewman forward hold the jib temporarily to windward.

Some skippers prefer not to hoist a jib until the mooring is cast off. This demands rapid hoisting. Occasionally a boat's bow, when leaving a mooring or during a tacking maneuver, will not come fully around. This is known as getting **"in irons."** Here are three remedial maneuvers. First, back the jib as above, which may suffice. If not, pull the tiller sharply toward the helmsman two or three times.

Finally, if a boat has gathered sternway, she may be brought "out of irons" by putting the tiller on the side of the boat toward which you wish to turn, causing the craft to push her stern toward the wind as she drifts astern. When she commences to pay off, bring the tiller sharply to the other side and the craft will usually fall off on the desired tack. In selecting the tack on which to leave mooring or float, be sure to allow plenty of sea room, thus avoiding a tack or jibe before your crew is fully organized to maneuver the boat.

Except when demonstrating helmsmanship, the experienced sailor should handle the mainsheet, and permit the new skipper to concentrate on what is known as reaching and tacking.

5. Reaching and Tacking

A boat on a reach is sailing toward a fixed point which is neither directly to windward nor dead to leeward. The skipper steers a definite course and sails are trimmed to conform to changes in wind direction in order to maintain maximum speed through the water. The sail is adjusted until it shows just a slight luff, or shaking, near the mast.

Left. Beam reaching, an 18' Interlake Sloop sails with sheets eased across the wind. Tell-tale on shroud indicates wind coming from abeam. (Courtesy, Customflex, Inc.) *Right.* In a good breeze, some craft will plane on a beam reach, and here a Thistle just commences to lift her bow as crew hikes out to windward. (Morris Rosenfeld photo)

If an instructor is present, he can give practical demonstrations of reaching and tacking before turning the tiller over to the inexperienced sailor.

Confining his first sails to protected waters, the new skipper should bring his boat into a position where the wind is coming from abeam, or at right angles to the boat's course. Now, looking ahead, he picks a landmark ashore or a buoy in the water—possibly a moored boat—and steers for this point. The helmsman, sighting over the bow, should be able to keep his craft headed quite close to the chosen point. He concentrates first on steering a course and lets the crew handle sail. If one person must both steer and handle sail, he should not be too concerned if his sail flaps a little at first, so long as he keeps heading for the selected point with the wind remaining approximately abeam.

After you have sailed for 100 yards or so, it is well to tack in order to remain fairly close to your starting point. A novice should not venture far from whence his sail started, and someone should always be watching from ashore or in a powerboat during early sailing. In lieu of such requisites, an experienced hand in another craft should be sailing nearby.

Prior to making the first tack, be sure the boat is under full control. A craft must have adequate speed, or **way,** to permit her to complete the tacking maneuver. Novice skippers, especially if winds are strong, tend to sail with the mainsail slacked off too far, and when the craft is brought toward the wind, she lacks enough speed to permit her to come head-to-wind and shift to the other tack. As a result, the boat either falls off on the same tack again, or, losing steerageway, becomes locked in irons head-to-wind.

Just before starting to tack, bring the helm slightly toward you. This will tend to give the boat "a rap full," or greater speed. Notice if your sails are full. If they are flapping or luffing, pull the sheet in until the flutter is gone.

The tacking maneuver is preceded by the command, "Ready about!" This warns the crew to be prepared. After noting the crew is ready, the skipper follows with a second command, "Hard-a-lee!" This is a contraction meaning "the helm is hard to leeward," or your helm has been pushed toward the leeward side. Sometimes called "putting the helm down," the tiller is pushed toward the sail with a decisive, but not violent, motion.

This turns the bow toward the wind. The sails will flutter shortly and the boom come amidships before crossing to the other side of the boat. Just before or as the boat comes head-to-wind, the skipper and crew, carefully avoiding interference with one another, cross to the opposite side of the boat. As the craft **pays off** (falls off) on the new tack, both skipper and crew need to be extremely alert. In tacking, the mainsheet of small boats often will have been slightly slacked, and the duty of the crew is to **trim** (haul in or adjust) the sail again

Left. **Playing with sheets and sails is never more important than in light winds, which this fleet of reaching Lightnings has encountered. (Courtesy, International Lightning Class Assn.)** *Right.* **In both beam or close reaching, balance and weight distribution, as well as sail trimming, can be important, as a fleet of International 12-footers at the Coast Guard Academy demonstrates. Note different sail trims, positions of crew, and angle of heel, all affecting speed.**

as the craft assumes her new course. The mainsheetman must be equally ready to slack sheets should a hard puff hit when tacking.

The helmsman must watch for two things when tacking. After a boat comes head-to-wind, a novice while changing his position is apt to bring his tiller back toward the center of the boat too soon, resulting in the craft getting into irons or even falling back on the same tack. If the fault of checking too soon is avoided, the skipper must not permit his boat to go too far around at the end of the tacking maneuver. Before starting to tack during early sails, skippers should look astern and pick out a point for which to sail after shifting, say from starboard to port, tacks. Then the helmsman should start to check his boat's turning movement at or just before her bow reaches such a point. If not checked in time, a lively sailer often will spin right around into a jibe after the tack, with the possible surprise of an unexpected swim for the crew.

A skipper in tacking should be careful to allow his craft to gather way after tacking. Sometimes a boat completes her tack but is checked too soon by her helmsman and hence loses, or fails to gather, speed. For a few seconds after tacking, the boat should be steered for a point slightly below the planned objective. As speed is gathered, one brings her up to the desired course.

When sailing a sloop, the tacking maneuver is only slightly complicated. Here, at the command "Ready about!" the crew uncleats the leeward jibsheet but holds the line taut in his hand until the boat comes head-to-wind. He now lets go this sheet, then pulls in and cleats the other rapidly. Some skippers prefer not to have the jib trimmed too flat immediately, in which case it is cleated a little slack and then trimmed taut when the boat has gathered way. If a boat is slow **in stays** (in-the-wind part of tacking), occasionally it is necessary to leave the jib trimmed to windward to push her bow around.

First sails should be confined to beam reaching across the wind, up and down a course near shore. After sailing this course and tacking several times, a skipper may commence experimenting with his sails controlling speed. Remember, the craft is sailing for a point which the skipper desires to reach as soon as possible. Note first that if the sail is trimmed too flat, the boat slows down. If slacked out too far, the sail flutters and again speed is lost. By playing main and jibsheets in and out gently, a skipper discovers the point, or combination of sail adjustments, where the boat sails fastest.

As confidence is acquired, a skipper should try handling not only his tiller but mainsheet, too, as through playing with sheets and moving the tiller at the same time one can both see and feel the reaction of the boat. When sailing a sloop, slacking or flattening jibsheets will affect speed noticeably. One-design boats on a beam or close reach are so equal in speed, the proper trimming of sheets will often add the extra speed—perhaps only five or so seconds a mile—to allow one craft to overtake or pull away from a rival when racing. Hence, never overlook the importance of playing the sails— particularly jibs, which may seem only small sails comparatively, but are in fact most important.

During early sails, a skipper may notice a tendency of his boat to edge to windward. When a craft behaves so, she is said to have a **weather helm.** If she tends to turn to leeward— which is apt to be rarer—it is termed a **leeward helm.** If not sure from the feel on the tiller, a skipper may test by lifting his hand off the helm in a light breeze and watching what happens.

A small amount of weather helm is desirable, as one will discover when learning to sail to windward. A strong weather

The importance of keeping the hull of light center-board craft level by means of hiking (keeping weight to windward) is demonstrated by Eric Olsen, another of the nation's best dinghy skippers, at the helm of a Flying Dutchman Junior on a reach. (Courtesy, Geveke & Co., Inc.)

helm can be a serious fault, very tiring in heavy winds for a skipper fighting constantly against the boat's desire to head into the wind. The remedy for a strong windward or leeward helm lies in adjusting sails and rigging. In reaching, or going to windward, a slight change in the trim of sails often will correct the balance. When reaching, a shift of the centerboard up or down may also counteract an undesirable helm.

If these adjustments fail to alter the situation, the answer is correcting the balance of the rigging, which sailors call **tuning.** Expert advice is recommended but, if unavailable, the novice may have to experiment. Perhaps the mast is **raked** (tipped) too far forward or aft. Possibly a jib or headstay is so taut the spar curves forward in a bow. Again, the trouble might lie in the shrouds; for if stays are set up more taut on one side than the other, the mast will be out of line, with the craft consequently sailing better on one tack than the opposite.

The aspects of tuning a sailboat are many and include ballast, cut of sails, trimming sails, rigging, and centerboard.

6. Tacking, Luffing, and Jibing

The previous chapter discussed tacking. The other turning maneuver is the **jibe** (also **gybe**), whereby the bow of the boat is turned away from, instead of toward, the wind to change from one course to another.

Before delving into jibing techniques, it is well to clarify two words frequently used in sailing which possess more than one meaning. "Tack" and "luff" can be used both as verbs and nouns, and to understand clearly their various meanings is important.

"Tack," as a noun has several meanings. The first applies to the corner of the sail where the luff joins the foot. This is the corner of a mainstail attached to the gooseneck at the joining of mast and boom, or the lower forward corner of any sail.

"Tack" is secondly used as a noun to describe a sailboat underway when the craft is said to be sailing on either the starboard or port tack. When the wind is blowing over the starboard side the craft is sailing on starboard tack; conversely, when the wind comes over the port rail, she is on port tack. Another way to determine the correct tack is to remember a boat is always on the tack opposite to the side on which she carries her main boom. This is true whether a boat is close-hauled, reaching, or running.

The third use of "tack" as a noun describes the completion of the tacking maneuver, as in speaking of a craft "having made a tack."

"Tack," as a verb, describes the action of changing course from starboard to port tack, or vice versa. This means the entire act of turning the boat's bow toward the direction from which the wind is blowing until the boom crosses the centerline of the boat and sails fill on the opposite side.

The tacking maneuver is the easiest, quickest, and safest way to shift from one tack to another. The reason is, the boat swings through an arc of relatively short radius and loses headway in so doing. As indicated earlier, a craft will make a better tack if given a rap-full before commencing to tack. When speed has been gathered the helm is put down, or pushed toward the sail. The boat, sails shaking, comes swiftly into the wind and the boom swings across the boat with crew

Left. In an intercollegiate regatta of Lehman Class Dinghies at Newport Harbor, Calif., No. 275 begins to *tack.* As skipper puts helm down, the bow turns toward the wind and sail starts to shake. At the same time, No. 102 carries a *luff* in her sail while trying to squeeze across starboard tack boats holding right of way. (Courtesy, Pacific Coast Intercollegiate Yacht Racing Assn.) *Right.* At other end of tacking maneuver, crew on 210 Class sloop No. 89 sailed by Bobby Coulson, famous racing skipper, pulls a Genoa jib around the mast after boom has crossed the centerline and the mainsail filled at the start of a windward leg following a beam reach.
(Courtesy, Gil Friedberg, Boston Globe)

simultaneously shifting to the new windward side. The good skipper sails his boat a bit free, lower than his preferred course, long enough for the craft to gain full headway before **pointing** (heading) as high as possible.

The pitfalls of tacking are few, but bear repetition. Most occur when the inexperienced skipper fails to allow his boat to complete her full swing and the craft stops part way, hanging in irons. This happens when the helmsman does not put his tiller down hard enough or his sails were not properly trimmed to gain the necessary momentum to carry the boat beyond head-to-wind.

To make a good tack, the skipper must have full control of his boat before the maneuver is started. The novice often fails to trim sails flat enough in a stiff breeze, with the result that the boat lacks sufficient momentum when the tack starts, and trouble ensues. While the action of putting the helm down should be decisive, it can be overdone, particularly when sailing light dinghy-type hulls, which are very fast in stays. To tack many boats by slamming the helm down will kill speed more than necessary, causing the boat to take a long time gathering headway on her new tack.

"Luff" is, likewise, a word of multiple meaning. The verb, "luff," means to turn in the direction from which the wind is blowing. When a boat starts to tack, she luffs. The word "luff" is not synonymous with tack, however, as craft may luff without tacking. A boat is luffing whenever she alters course toward the wind, but is tacking only when the luff is carried so far the boom crosses the centerline. When a sail shakes, or flaps, it luffs; this is the second use of the word as a verb.

"Luff" as a noun describes the maneuver a boat makes by turning toward the wind, and this type of luff can be a very important tactical maneuver in racing. As defined in Chapter Two, "luff" denotes the leading edge of a sail. The third use of "luff" as a noun describes the flapping of a sail. When the sail's leading edge shakes or flutters, the boat is said to be carrying a luff in her sail.

"Jibe" (gybe) describes a second method of turning to change from one tack to another. Here a boat is turned away from the wind, as opposed to tacking. Jibing has greater pitfalls than tacking, and these should be understood before jibes are attempted. While requiring skipper and crew to be more alert, jibes often are made to sound much more difficult and dangerous than they actually are.

As learned in tacking, a boat loses momentum by turning into the wind. In jibing, conversely, a boat gathers speed as she turns away from the wind and swings through an arc of much greater radius than when tacking. The skipper prepares the crew by his command "Stand by to jibe," or "Ready to jibe." He should ascertain that all gear, as well as his crew, is ready before giving the command of execution "Jibe!" or "Jibe Ho!" When boat and crew are prepared, a jibe is rarely dangerous or difficult.

In executing a jibe, the bow is swung away from the direction of the wind by pulling the tiller to windward; another way of expressing this is to put the helm up, i.e., pull it toward the helmsman. Notice that this is contrary to the action used in tacking, where the helmsman puts the tiller down, or to leeward. As the bow swings away from the wind the mainsheet is hauled in slowly, thus flattening the angle of the sail. If a boat is sailing close-hauled before jibing, this may be unnecessary.

When jibing, as with tacking, skipper and crew move to the

opposite side of the boat when, or just before, the boom crosses the centerline. It is extremely important for the crew to be to windward as the sails fill, for the skipper or crew, handling the mainsheet, must be prepared to slack sheets rapidly to check a strong tendency of the boat to turn sharply into the wind.

Knockdowns frequently follow the completion of a jibe as a result of failure to ease the mainsheet or shift the crew's weight to windward soon enough. In these circumstances, a sailboat may capsize, break a spar, or carry away gear. Due to increased momentum during a jibe, the action of the boom in crossing the boat is always sharper than when tacking, thus placing heavier strain on gear and rigging. If a boat has running backstays, the leeward stay, shortly to become the windward one, must always be set up taut prior to the boom's

Left. Beetle Cat, very popular, small edition of famous Cape Cod catboats and a good, able craft for the windy, rough waters of Buzzards and Narragansett Bays, carries the old-fashioned gaff rig. Hoisting sail by hoops around the mast makes for a less-efficient luff, which is the most important part of a sail. (Courtesy, Concordia Co., Inc.) *Right.* Luffing into Luff! No. 6609 turns toward the wind, with sails shaking, to squeeze by leeward starting-line marker in a Lightning Class race. Timed too early, boat at right has jibed to make another attempt, and No. 6699 also may have to jibe. (Morris Rosenfeld photo)

swing across the boat. It usually is advisable to have both backstays set up until the jibe has been completed, then quickly slack off the new leeward stay.

The word "jibe" also is used as a noun in the sense that a boat is sailing on the starboard or port jibe. This usage is correct, though not as common as starboard or port tack, but applies only when boats are sailing free—usually either broad reaching or running.

Whenever tacking or jibing, crews should be alert to keep clear of the boom crossing the boat. The larger a craft the more important this warning becomes, for crew members have been swept overboard, stunned, or knocked out by the boom at the exact moment when their services were most needed.

7. Landing and Mooring

Every true sailor takes pride in his seamanship, which is never more on public display than when picking up a mooring or landing at a wharf. If your boat is moored in a harbor, there unquestionably are dozens of critical eyes watching every time you pick up a mooring, and even more will be scrutinizing a landing at a public or yacht club float.

Left. A Flying Dutchman Junior sailing on a beam reach demonstrates the ease of controlling speed by slacking sheets when approaching mooring or float. (Courtesy, Geveke & Co.) *Right.* Turnabouts, tied rail-to-rail with slatting sails, confront skippers attempting windward landings with a real problem, even though craft are head-to-wind. (Courtesy, National Turnabout Assn.)

Before undertaking to sail to windward and run before the wind, new skippers must learn to make a proper landing and to pick up a mooring. The first sail or two should be limited to beam reaching over short courses, with practice in tacking at the end of each leg. If winds are not too strong, or if a good instructor is on board, it is advisable by the second or third sail to practice jibing. Tacking and jibing are both needed when approaching a mooring or float.

Picking Up a Mooring
Moorings actually are heavy anchors or weights to which

boats are **moored** (secured) by means of chain and rope. They are marked by mooring buoys or floats commonly referred to as "moorings."

Picking up a mooring is easier than landing at a float, as moorings almost always can be approached with some freedom of action on a beam reach; floats may be crowded, or located so that an extremely difficult leeward landing cannot be avoided.

In tacking his boat, the skipper will have gained some idea of how far she will shoot when headed directly into the wind. This helps greatly in judging the distance from which to attempt to make the mooring. Moorings should always be approached on a beam reach from far enough to leeward so that when a boat shoots into the wind her way will be sufficient to reach the buoy. Too much speed results in overshooting; too little, in falling short. Nothing brings louder chortles from spectators than the skipper who overshoots his mooring and runs into the boat anchored ahead, or whose craft ends up in irons for lack of proper way.

A fair rule for light displacement boats is to plan the approach on a course about 2 boat lengths to leeward of the mooring. For heavier keel craft the distance should be further to leeward, as they carry momentum longer; shoal draft, centerboard boats quickly lose headway when shot into the wind. Because variations in wind strength and direction also must be taken into account, a significant advantage of the beam reach approach is greater facility in controlling speed by slacking or trimming sheets.

The idea is to reduce speed to provide just enough way to shoot the mooring. When directly to leeward of the buoy, the craft is headed into the wind to bring the mooring under her bow. Once the mooring has been picked up, sheets are slacked off further to prevent sails from filling prior to the opportunity for lowering.

If the boat is a sloop, she probably has a forward deck from which a man lying prone near the bow can grasp the buoy easily and pull the mooring aboard. On high-freeboard craft, boathooks are used to pick up the float. In small open boats of the dinghy type, the float must be brought alongside amidships or further aft when sailing single-handed.

Only after a skipper has made enough moorings to know the

Left. Though these intercollegiate racing dinghies have made windward landings, damage to hulls and sails is threatened by leaving craft with mainsails hoisted. (Official U.S. Navy photo) **Right.** Two Dyer (Class D) Dinghies have been brought head-to-wind alongside a float rather than head-on, although sheet on No. 132 should have been slacked out farther.

reactions of his boat under various conditions should he attempt to lower his mainsail while shooting the mooring. It makes a smart bit of seamanship to shoot a craft into the wind, drop sails, and have just enough way to reach the mooring. Conversely, it is most embarrassing for a skipper to lower sails, miss the mooring, and perhaps drift into craft anchored nearby.

Neat seamanship when picking up moorings will win admiration from the saltiest sailors. Harold S. "Mike" Vanderbilt, three-time defender of the America's Cup, could shoot these 130' yachts, displacing 140 tons, into the wind and stop dead in the water as the mooring was hooked. Sailors would nod admiringly as Vanderbilt thus brought *Ranger* or *Rainbow* alongside his big power yacht *Vara* without scratching the paint on either craft.

Windward Landing

When approaching a float to tie up a boat, the helmsman must bear in mind that wind variations are accentuated close to shore. Skippers cannot predict the actions of other boats approaching or leaving piers, hence speed should be reduced and caution exercised.

Since small boats usually are secured to landings by a single painter and lie with their bows to the wind, helmsmen should plan always to have their craft reach the float head-to-wind. This is called making a **windward landing**, that is, against a "shore lying to windward," which might be a float, pier, beach, anchored boat, or mooring. Good seamen make windward landings whenever possible.

As with picking up a mooring, the best approach is a beam reach with the mainsail luffing halfway to the leech, for the last 100′ or so, to reduce speed if the breeze has any strength. A beam reach facilitates slacking or trimming sails in shifts of wind direction and velocity which prevail near shore. Landing at floats, slips, or docks (technically, the water space between piers) often involves maneuvering into narrow berths between other craft. Caution is important, but enough speed should be retained for steerage way, allowing a boat to coast by for a second try if conditions are not right. Whenever possible the preferred landing is to bring a boat, when luffed head-to-wind, along the side of a float rather than head-on into a landing.

When approaching any fixed object, the alert skipper makes certain his sheets have been overhauled to run easily through the blocks to allow rapid trimming or slacking without jamming. Sails even can act as air brakes when making a landing by having the crew push the boom out until the sail is completely backwinded. There is small excuse for over-shooting with a resultant crash landing.

A certain amount of practice naturally is required to perfect technique. Windward landings should first be practiced at a float not crowded with other craft. The size and type of boat will make slight variations of approach advisable.

When a craft has a foredeck a crew member is stationed forward, holding the stay with painter in hand, ready to jump on the float and help retard the boat's momentum by fending off. Don't expect a crew to do the whole job of stopping a boat—possibly to risk breaking a leg by attempting to hold off a fast traveling boat with his feet while seated on the bow!

In dinghy types without foredeck, the boat's stability is endangered by anyone forward of the mast, so reduction of the craft's way before reaching the landing is vital. If done properly, just as the boat's forward progress almost halts, it is possible to swing the bow off enough (with sails well slacked) to permit crew or skipper to grasp the pier as the craft comes almost parallel to the dock. Care must be exercised not to gather new momentum during this maneuver.

Landings often are simplified if someone is standing on the pier to whom a line can be thrown before the boat reaches the float.

As soon as a craft is secured, sails should be lowered. Even with her sheets slacked well off, the wind tends to catch the sails of a boat tied to a float, causing her to sail short distances in one direction or another, bumping against other boats or the pier. Even if she has a protective rub rail or the floats possess bumpers, serious damage may result to someone's craft. There may be occasional excuse for leaving sails hoisted at a

Dinghies at U.S. Coast Guard Academy float illustrate problems which occur when wind conditions are not ideal. Boats 9 to 22 had to dock under conditions approaching, though not exactly duplicating those of a leeward landing. (Official photo, U.S. Coast Guard Academy)

pier if immediate departure impends. There is no excuse, however, for keeping sails hoisted for prolonged periods, or when skipper and crew leave the proximity of the craft. This not only is bad seamanship, but disregard for the property of others and neglect of your own, for a sail is damaged far more by slatting a few minutes than from many hours of sailing.

Leeward Landing

Many docks and floats permit tying up to more than one side, so even with the wind blowing against or parallel to the offshore side, it is possible to pick a spot on the end or opposite side where a safe windward landing can be made.

There may be rare conditions, however, due to wind, shoal water, or crowding of boats at a float, when the only alternative remaining is to make the final approach from directly to windward. This is called a **leeward landing,** that is, against a "lee shore," and is to be avoided by good sailors as a plague.

When a leeward landing is unavoidable, there will be small choice of approach or tack, and the boom and sail will project over the float when the craft comes alongside. The best procedure is still a beam reach with an approach parallel to the face of the float.

In this case the boat must be luffed away from, instead of toward the float, opposite the desired landing spot. The sails of small boats should be backwinded by holding the boom forward, thus stopping the boat and causing her to make stern-way. At this point the tiller should be moved to windward, steering the stern into the landing, and the centerboard should be raised, allowing the bow to fall off toward the float. Smartly executed, this maneuver makes a reasonably satisfactory landing. Naturally the beam reach approach must be fairly close to the pier to permit the craft to back in properly upon losing headway. Under no circumstances should inexperienced sailors attempt leeward landings.

Another solution to a leeward landing problem—more appealing to the novice as well as to others when float space is extremely limited—is to bring a craft in under bare poles. This means dropping sails and permitting the action of the wind on the hull to sail the boat into a float. Considerable caution needs to be exercised in picking the best available spot and in reducing speed to the barest minimum. In a rough sea, a bare-pole landing can be nearly as difficult as a leeward one under full sail.

While leeward landings may be necessary under certain circumstances, wind and water conditions could cause almost suicidal damage to hull and spars of your, or someone else's, boat. A recommended alternative is to pick up a mooring, or throw out an anchor near the pier, and go ashore in a power or rowboat.

Anchoring techniques come under the general subject of ground tackle, but the maneuver of bringing a boat to anchor is almost identical with picking up a mooring; a beam reach approach, a shoot into the wind clear of anchored boats, and finally, when headway has been lost, the anchor dropped from the boat as sails are lowered. The crew handling the anchor works on the foredeck, making sure that anchor line is attached and flaked down in long loops to run free, without kinks or bights in which an arm or leg can be caught to pull a man overboard. Surprisingly, anchors are sometimes tossed overboard without rode secured.

8. Sailing to Windward

Beating, sailing to windward, tacking a boat to weather—terms used almost interchangeably—is the fine art of sailing. Yet, a moderate degree of proficiency can be acquired by nearly anyone who sails. Many become reasonably expert, but it is reserved for relatively few persons to develop that gifted touch at windward sailing which marks the great helmsman—the Bus Mosbacher, Artie Knapp, Ted Wells, Lowell North, or Ted Hood.

Left. **Three Blue Jays in a row, sailing to windward. Careful scrutiny will detect the jib on No. 168 is starting to luff and her lesser angle of heel hints she may be pointing too high. (Morris Rosenfeld photo)** *Right.* **A well-trimmed and balanced Hodgdon 21-footer on the wind needs only a light touch on the tiller in her roomy cockpit.**

Basic problems of windward sailing should be reviewed before discussing the fine points of sailing to windward—those elusive qualities called "feel" and "touch" which every skipper hopes to master in order to become truly skillful.

As you know, boats cannot sail directly into the wind because sails commence to flutter along the luff at a point about 45° from the direction of the wind. Therefore, to reach a destination to windward, a boat must sail a zigzag, tacking course, heading as high as possible with advantage and climbing to windward with each tack. Heading to windward with advan-

Left. **A Mobjack sailing on the edge of a light breeze with the proper balance for a centerboard boat—an angle of heel which keeps leeward rail well out of the water.** (**Courtesy, East Coast Boats**) *Right.* **A novice skipper properly sails a Tech Dinghy by watching the luff of well-fitting sail.** (**Courtesy of M.I.T.**)

tage means a boat is sailing on the edge of the wind (just as close to the wind as possible) while still maintaining reasonable headway. This is accomplished by trimming the mainsail until the boom is over the stern quarter and the sail's leech is just beginning to straighten out due to the downward pull of the mainsheet.

The basic difference between sailing a boat to windward and sailing free, or off the wind, is that, in beating, the sail is kept trimmed to a close-hauled position and course altered to follow the shifts and variations of the breeze. In reaching and running, it will be recalled, the course is constant and sails are hauled or slacked to obtain the most effective trim and speed.

To sail to windward with advantage, the skipper alters his helm with very small and easy movements designed to keep his craft sailing on the very edge of the wind without losing speed. When her sail starts to luff, it warns he is in danger of sailing too close to the wind, which is called **pinching**. On sloops, the jib is usually trimmed to luff before the mainsail does, and the jib is the sail a helmsman watches. Skippers must be careful not to confuse a lifting of the mainsail, caused

57

by backwind from the jib, with a true luffing of the sail due to pinching. In catboats, the lift in a mainsail means the craft, if properly trimmed, is sailing on the wind's edge.

A craft may be pinched either by trimming too flat or carrying too great a luff in the sail. When sails are trimmed rather flat, a skipper must learn to gauge his speed rather than watch for the sail to luff. If his boat tends to slow up, then even though sails may not flutter, she is pointing too high for the best advantage. One should bear off, or slack sheets, possibly both. It is well to recall that hull shapes and the cut of sails make some boats more close-winded than others.

When a boat is sailing **on the wind** (to windward), sheets are never slacked to make sails conform to variations in wind direction. Sheets are slacked only when necessary to spill wind from a sail, due to a stronger wind than the boat can stand (possibly avoiding a capsizal) and to make small adjustments in the trim of sail to balance the boat properly, usually as the result of changes in the strength, NOT THE DIRECTION, of the breeze.

The primary concern here is sailing rather than racing; yet, it is wise to cultivate the same proficiencies of sailing to windward which would be useful in racing. The performance of a well-equipped and maintained boat when racing to windward relies heavily on the ability of the helmsman. It is the skipper's skill which gets a boat to windward fastest, while in sailing off the wind the trimming of sails becomes most important.

The following portions of this chapter are taken largely from the pamphlet, "Sailing to Windward," which the author wrote with Lieutenant Commander Walter C. Wood, USCGR, for instruction of regular and reserve cadets of the U. S. Coast Guard Academy during World War II. Based on previous material used at M.I.T., these sections explain Jack Wood's ideas on the use of one's senses and faculties, which have helped to develop many top college skippers.

Feel, Sometimes Called "Touch"

Those elusive qualities, known to the sailing fraternity as "feel" or "touch," are difficult to describe to the novice, yet make the difference between the average and skillful skipper. Beyond suggesting that a thing called "feel" exists to aid a skipper in getting the best performance from his boat, some instructors have trouble elaborating on the theme. Crack skippers know when a boat is going well, but when questioned will often answer, "You either have 'the touch' or you don't."

This implies an inherited quality not easily acquired by practice and original thought by the pupil. Jack Wood of M.I.T. refuses to subscribe to this mysterious theory. His contention, based on extensive teaching, is that any alert novice can quickly become a proficient helmsman possessing "feel" by practicing the use of other faculties rather than simply watching a sail's luff when sailing to windward.

Most novices are taught, quite properly, to sail to windward by sight alone. With the sail trimmed to the proper position over the stern quarter they are told to watch the flutter at the luff of a jib or mainsail. When the sail quivers one bears away, and if the sail looks too firm or hard then one turns the boat to windward until such flutter just appears. Granting such procedure is proper for beginners, skippers should quickly learn this is only one of many indications to be observed in sailing a boat most efficiently to windward.

Left. **Sailing a Firefly Dinghy single-handed demands that John Lawson use his senses of hearing, touch, and balance in addition to sight. Jib is just lifting. (Courtesy, M.I.T.)** *Right.* **This Jolly Boat appears to have just a slight windward helm, permitting skipper to sail with hiking stick (tiller extension) and use his weight to balance boat easily on the wind. (Photo by Clifton Feero)**

Of the five major senses one must use three—sight, hearing, and touch—as well as that more elusive factor, a sense of balance. Proper practice in developing the senses of hearing, touch, and balance can do much to augment the sense of sight and improve ability to gain the most speed from a boat when sailing to windward.

Before amplifying how each sense helps, the aim in sailing to windward bears repeating. The problem is to sail that course which will gain the greatest distance to windward in the shortest time—sailing wide of the wind and fast, or close to the wind but slower.

The hull or sails, the weather or water conditions, may provide different answers under each existing circumstance to be weighed before reaching final conclusions.

Sight

With the eyes one watches the luff of a sail to note the degree it is luffing. This may not, however, show whether the boat is moving through the water as fast as she should for greatest efficiency. Speed may be determined by watching the water slipping along the rail, being thrown away from the bow, or leaving the aft part of the hull in quarter wave and wake. Sight also permits comparisons of speed by using nearby boats, buoys, or marks on shore.

Since the most efficient point of sailing is when the sail is full, a few compass degrees away from the luffing point, watching the luff can be of value only in gauging the angle of the boat from the wind. Occasional luffs will check this point.

In strong winds, sailing a boat with a considerable luff in her sail is advisable in order to keep the craft on a more even keel. Here, a luffing sail has small value as an indication of speed; so the angle of heel, as indicated by the distance of the water from the leeward rail, becomes a more accurate yardstick of how close to the wind to sail. Nearly all boats when sailing to windward have a definite angle of heel at which they travel fastest. With any excessive angle, boats slow down and make too much leeway. Centerboard and chine-built craft are designed to sail best to windward when their angle of heel is very slight.

Hearing

One may wonder how hearing possibly can aid in determining how close to the wind a boat may sail with efficiency. Yet, when sailing at night, sails are not visible, and a skillful skipper can still sail well to windward with the help of his ears. As a craft edges closer to the wind, the helmsman hears the sail slides or rigging rattle ever so lightly to indicate a luffing sail. Maybe the rhythmic swish of water from the bow wave becomes fainter as it gurgles at a reduced speed along

Left. A Lightning is kept on her feet, or in balance, by carrying a sizeable luff in the mainsail during a stiff breeze. Hiking by crew, although not in the most approved fashion, helps. (Morris Rosenfeld photo) *Right.* Leslie Goodwin, veteran Buzzards Bay shipbuilder, sails a Marlin to windward, as a good skipper should, with his face well clear of wind disturbances caused by sails and rigging. (Courtesy, Cape Cod Shipbuilding Co.)

the hull by his side. His immediate reaction should be to bear away from the wind. While hearing may be most important in night sailing, it can be developed as an important asset at all times.

Touch

Touch generally is associated with the feel of the hand upon the tiller but has other important aspects—the feel of wind against one's face and the pressure of one's body against the seat and rail—aiding the sense of balance. In a breeze of steady strength, pressure of the tiller in the hand is relatively constant. If the boat is balanced properly, with a slight windward helm, the tiller presses to leeward. As the boat is turned closer to the wind, the pressure diminishes. By bearing away, increased pressure is felt.

Changes of wind intensity also affect the feel on a tiller, as more pressure is required to prevent the boat from rounding, or heading up, in a puff. As a boat slows, water pressure against the rudder fades and the helm feels slack. These signs, even without one's sight and hearing, would be clues helpful in sailing an efficient windward course.

Balance

Through a sense of balance, one feels slight changes in the heel of the boat. The delicate balancing mechanism of the ear, assisted by changes in pressure of one's body against the seat or rail, aid in detecting slight variations of heel which, with sound and feel, help determine the proper windward course to sail.

The feeling of the breeze against one's face gives an instant check on the force of the wind and, to a lesser degree, on its direction. As long as the wind blows steadily against the face, one knows a puff of wind is present, but if the face grows warmer one realizes the wind has died somewhat. The extent to which this feeling of wind intensity can be developed, once one has learned to observe it, is remarkable.

After learning to sail with a fair degree of competence, an easy way to develop the senses is to blindfold the eyes when sailing. Of course there must be a co-skipper to pilot the craft away from boats and obstacles, but blindfold sailing to windward using hearing, touch, and balance will perfect the art of climbing to windward. John B. Herreshoff, founder of the famous Bristol, R. I., concern which built 5 America's Cup defenders designed by his brother, Nathanael, was totally blind from the age of 14 and yet an excellent skipper.

In attempting the blindfold experiment, the co-skipper should watch and trim sails, advising the helmsman when he is sailing too high until the latter has learned to interpret correctly the tiny indications of wind intensity, sound, and touch.

This blindfold experiment should be attempted only in a moderate-sized boat, which is neither too quick nor too sluggish. Dinghies react too quickly for one to develop these senses well when blindfolded, but similar practice in dinghy types may be achieved by studiously looking away from the sail, or momentarily closing the eyes. The luff must be checked periodically to confirm one's position relative to the wind.

Some skippers grasp a tiller like a vise and glue their eyes to the luff as if to make the boat submit to their will and sail any course the helmsman desires. This is tiring and inefficient. Such skippers will profit by learning to relax and develop other senses to relieve strain on eyes and body. Sailing for

A Flying Dutchman, Olympic two-man boat, shows the slot, or funnel, between genoa jib and leeward side of a mainsail. Crew is using a "flying trapeze" to get weight out to windward in balancing boat. (Courtesy, George D. O'Day Associates)

pleasure should be relaxing. A skipper too dependent on watching the luff cannot search for puffs of wind on the water to windward. When racing, a skipper needs to use his eyes to keep track of nearby competitors while still sailing competently.

If one constantly practices use of all senses, sailing to windward can become as instinctive as walking. To sail by watching the luff alone is equivalent to walking with one's eyes following each step. Responding to changes in the wind's strength and direction should become as normal as climbing stairs.

In analyzing the reaction of a boat as she edges toward the wind, one notes how, in turning closer to the breeze, her hull starts to lose its angle of heel. This action often occurs before the sail commences to luff. In strong winds, it happens when the sails have lost their grip on the wind—the smooth flow of air which produces the propelling drive.

In an airplane wing, loss of grip or lift indicates the "burble point" at which the smooth flow of air over the surface is interrupted. When a sail luffs, this "burble point" has been passed and the flow of wind interrupted so the sail no longer performs most efficiently. If a skipper can determine just when the sail is about to luff and not permit the boat to edge any closer to the wind, then the craft is sailing close to her point of greatest efficiency. This, one tries to determine by senses other than sight.

Starting at the point of sailing where the sail luffs slightly, if one bears away from the wind a boat increases her heel somewhat. Within approximately 10° of turn, a boat assumes an angle of heel which increases very slightly in turning further away from the wind. The critical point, where a boat is in delicate balance between maximum angle of heel and a tendency to right herself, appears the point of greatest efficiency. One can sail on this point by balance just as one can sail by watching a luff. When watching the luff, one has visual indication of the wind's effect upon a sail, while with the angle of heel, or balance, the resultant effect of the wind on speed and the boat's angle of heel are the indicators.

There are times, particularly in very light air, when only by watching the sail may a skipper be assured of his boat's position relative to the wind, as no change in heel can be noted. Occasionally, even the sail may not luff, so one must depend on smoke, wind vanes, or streamers to obtain the wind direction in order to decide the best angle at which to sail most efficiently. Then a skipper should choose his position at some point where he can watch the sails and still feel on his face the relative wind, undisturbed by downdrafts from the sail or cockpit **coamings** (rail).

For this reason, the best spot for a skipper is at the forward end of the tiller, on or close to the windward rail, with his face high enough to be free from any obstructions disturbing the wind's flow. In extremely light airs where it is of greatest importance to watch sails, particularly the jib, a leeward position may be desirable; but a novice helmsman will do well to confine his sailing to the windward side. The leeward position can prove dangerous in a small open boat if a puff of wind strikes suddenly.

Boats where a large overlapping or genoa jib is the dominant sail provide another exception to the rule that the skipper should sit to windward. Here, a funnel is formed between the curves of mainsail and big jib to make a leeward position advantageous in detecting slight luffs of the jib not visible from the windward side. This slot provides a most sensitive gauge of any changes in wind velocity, but not of shifts in direction. Craft carrying large genoas often are sailed in strong winds with sizeable luffs or backwind in their mainsails, so helmsmen prefer to sail entirely by these big jibs. Most skippers of small boats prefer to sit to windward where their weight is an important balancing factor in stiff winds.

To recapitulate the value of the senses in tabular form, note what happens when one sails too close to the wind:

1. *Sight*—one sees:
    (a) the jib or mainsail luff;
    (b) the leeward side rise out of the water.
2. *Balance*—one feels:
    (a) the bow wave or wake diminish;
    (b) the boat start to right herself.
3. *Hearing*—one hears:
    (a) reduced gurgle at bow and side;
    (b) rhythm of wave formation striking bow slow down;
    (c) sail slide or rigging noises.
4. *Feeling*—one feels:
    (a) reduced pressure of the body against seat or rail which indicates righting;
    (b) rush of water by rudder transmitted to the hand through the tiller;
    (c) reduced pressure on the tiller;
    (d) lack of wind against the face, indicating a slowing down of the boat or a slackening of the wind.

9. Running and Broad Reaching

A boat sailing with the wind blowing from astern or across her aft quarter is said to be running before the wind or sailing on a broad reach. The demarcation between a run and the broader reaches is so hazy, many authorities make almost no distinction between the two. This writer prefers to say a boat is running when the wind is coming from within one compass point (11¼°) either side of directly astern, and broad reaching whenever the breeze is blowing from other points abaft the beam.

Left. **A Hustler Class catboat running before the wind with centerboard raised and masthead fly indicating wind is coming from very slightly to windward of dead astern. (Photo by Clifton Feero)** *Right.* **Flatties run before the wind on opposite tacks with No. 272's sails threatening to jibe. (Courtesy, International Flattie Class Y.R.A.)**

Whether broad reaching or running, the principle used whenever sailing free—that is, other than to windward—applies, and a boat is held to a specified course with sails adjusted to gain maximum speed. Though subject to minor variations due to temporary course changes, shifts of wind, or tidal conditions, sails on runs and the broader reaches are

Left. Eric Olsen sails a Flying Dutchman Jr. wing-and-wing with boat intentionally heeled slightly to windward to bring center of effort of sails over hull, balance helm, and increase speed. (Courtesy, Geveke & Co., Inc.) *Right.* The America's Cup defender Columbia broad reaching with a cross-cut spinnaker. Upper cloths meet or cross at angle. (Morris Rosenfeld photo, courtesy, Fred E. Hood)

slacked nearly as far out as they will go. In light airs it often is necessary to hold or tie the boom to prevent the spar slatting back and forth. This may be accomplished by a crew member leaning gently against the boom, or by means of a **guy** (rope or wire used for steadying purposes) led forward. A **vang** (rope or wire leading from boom to hull) holds a boom down in strong winds.

Centerboards usually are raised completely unless needed to assist in steering, and leeward running backstays are run forward. When the reach is less broad, with the wind, for example, on the aft quarter, or 45° from dead astern, sails will be trimmed somewhat flatter with less tendency to slat, but more centerboard may be required to prevent sliding to leeward of the desired course.

The great danger in sailing directly before the wind is the unexpected jibe. If the helmsman is not careful, he may start unconsciously sailing **by the lee.** This means the wind is tending to blow from the same side on which the sail is carried, or from leech to luff, rather than vice versa. The helmsman may be warned of the danger of jibing by looking occasionally at the masthead **fly** (wind direction pennant), thus avoiding serious trouble. If the fly points directly toward the bow, skippers need be alert, especially if seas and wind cause a craft to **yaw** (steer with difficulty). If the pennant indicates the breeze is coming from the same side as the boom, they are warned to watch for and prevent an accidental jibe.

In a race, to retain right of way over a competitor or avoid double jibes near a mark, craft are sometimes sailed purposely by the lee; but otherwise, the risks are not warranted and the skipper should alter course by pointing a bit higher, or make a planned jibe. This is accomplished by heading up slightly as the sail is hauled in. When the boom approaches the center-line the skipper puts the helm up for a jibe, after which the crew slacks the mainsheet quickly. The jib often will jibe of its own accord, but will need to be trimmed from the leeward side as the maneuver is completed.

It is possible to sail wing-and-wing when directly before the wind with the jib trimmed, or poled out to windward. Wing-and-wing sailing is slightly more usual in larger boats, especially schooners and ketches.

When sailing before the wind, jibs, due to being hoisted on sloping stays, cannot be used effectively. A substitute sail known as a **spinnaker,** which can be set at right angles to the wind, is more efficient. These glamorous sails made of light-weight cloth are used primarily by racing boats, but can be carried when day sailing or cruising if one is anxious to reach his destination quickly. Most inquiring youngsters want to experiment with spinnakers as soon as they graduate from a catboat to a sloop. Spinnakers on catboats are a rarity, although these sails are used presently on Turnabouts and some other training boats.

Spinnakers, along with reaching jibs and staysails, are known as **light sails.** They are designed to increase speed of a boat before or across the wind by means of their larger areas and extremely light weight. Methods of accelerating speed before the wind are desirable because, contrary to popular belief, a boat is on her slowest point of sailing when running and broad reaching.

Sailors learned years ago to add additional canvas to speed their craft. The studding sails of clipper ships proved one answer by setting extra canvas on extensions of the regular

Left. Alert spinnaker watching and trimming are needed as crew rivets eyes on a Lightning kite. (Courtesy, International Lightning Class) **Right.** Hodgdon 21-footer on a run shows spinnaker rig with guys running fore and aft from pole, sheet led outside shrouds and under main boom, and boom lift with bridle on a spinnaker pole.

spars, or yards. Development of the fore and aft rig with growth of competitive sailing during the mid-19th century produced the racing spinnaker—a light sail held out to windward by a pole or boom from the mast.

Early spinnakers resembled large, lightweight jibs called ballooners. They had narrow heads, roped or wired luffs, and free leeches from which the wind could escape. Today, these are called single-luff spinnakers.

As masts grew taller, and **foretriangles** (area between mast, headstay, and foredeck) became smaller with the advent of jibheaded mainsails, a double-luff spinnaker was developed. In effect, this was sewing two spinnakers together, leech-to-leech. In the early 1930s a much publicized spinnaker of this type, cut fuller than usual, was devised by the famous sailmaker, Ernest Ratsey, and was carried successfully on his small cruising cutter *Golliwog*, which gave her name to this type of sail.

Thus began a competition in designing bigger and better spinnakers which still continues, with notable contributions from Prescott Wilson, Harry Nye, Ted Hood, Wally Ross, and a Frenchman named Herbulot. By the time of the

America's Cup matches of 1934 and 1937 in Class J sloops, these spinnakers had also taken the name of **parachute spinnakers,** with *Rainbow, Weetamoe, Yankee,* and *Ranger* carrying spinnakers of an area approaching 16,000 sq. ft. This was equivalent to the measured sail (mainsail and foretriangle) of the 1903 Cup defender, *Reliance,* a craft 15′ longer, even without her tremendous bowsprit, than the Class J sloops.

World War II experience in making nylon parachutes enabled sailmakers to develop still larger spinnakers by cutting the upper part of the sail to resemble a parachute. The Hood cross-cut spinnaker is an example.

A spinnaker is hoisted by a halyard to a sheave usually placed just above the point where the jibstay or headstay attaches to the mast, although masthead spinnakers are carried on some boats. One tack—parachute spinnaker tacks and clews are interchangeable—is attached to the outer end of a pole whose inboard end fits into a socket or hooks onto the mast. The sheet leads from the other tack or clew around the jibstay and leeward shroud, under the boom, to a position which permits trimming from the cockpit. A similar sheet, called a guy, is secured where the tack is attached to the spinnaker pole, and leads aft to windward outside the shrouds.

By playing—that is, hauling and slacking—both sheet and guy, the spinnaker is trimmed forward or aft, flat or billowing, as required. The object is to trim the pole as far aft as possible while still keeping this light cloth kite filled with air. Trim of spinnakers often is helped by a forward guy leading from the center of the pole to foredeck and thence aft. Sail trimmers watch the luff for the first sign of a break (luffing or caving-in). The sail is most effective when kept full, right on the edge of breaking.

The helmsman's job is to avoid an erratic course which would make spinnaker trimming difficult, and he can help keep a spinnaker full, particularly on a beam reach, by alertly watching the sail—as he would a jib luff when beating to windward—and bearing away slightly whenever the kite starts to break. His main job is to steer a relatively straight course, however, and let the crew adjust the spinnaker for greatest effectiveness. In some small boats the helmsman can play a sheet or guy, but spinnaker trimming often is a full-time job requiring both hands of one man (and sometimes two men).

The spinnaker is a fascinating sail to the inquisitive sailor. After becoming experienced, a skipper may experiment by detaching this sail from its pole and holding a sheet in each hand, much as Great Grandfather drove a team of horses, to try to keep the sail drawing. When racing, the rules forbid using spinnakers detached from poles except while jibing.

Interchangeable guys and sheets greatly simplify the problem of jibing modern spinnakers. The technique calls for removing the pole from the mast, pulling the spar inboard, attaching the clew, unsnapping the tack, and finally placing the new inboard end on the mast. Spinnaker poles have identical fittings on each end.

When the operation is completed, the sheet has become the guy and vice versa. Luff and leech also are reversed, technically, though luff is the common designation today for both outer edges, and the foot sometimes is called the skirt. Most of the jibing maneuver should be accomplished before the main boom crosses the boat, as once the wind catches the portion of the spinnaker hitherto to leeward of the mainsail, it becomes much harder to control the sail.

If a boat has an old-fashioned spinnaker, the method of jibing depends on the location of its halyard block. If the block is placed above the headstay the spinnaker must be detached from the pole, carried around the headstay and secured again to the pole, which has been brought across the boat. If located below the stay, then spinnaker and pole usually can be flipped from one side to the other with a prayer that one's precautions will prevent sheet, guy, and sail from ending up in a tangle. Whenever any type of spinnaker is jibed, the skipper should make sure the crew is organized with gear and sheets ready before ordering the maneuver.

Because the slowest point of sailing is directly before the wind, boats often broad reach back and forth at a wide angle to the wind with a series of jibes, instead of running straight for their objective. This is known as jibing or tacking down the wind, sometimes called **beating to leeward.**

Broad reaching without a spinnaker does not vary greatly from running, except that the danger of the unexpected jibe is nearly eliminated. Sails will be slacked—the distance depending on how far off the wind the course lies—and the jib may be somewhat more effective while both sails are trimmed just hard enough to avoid much flutter, thus indicating they are giving maximum efficiency.

The closer to the wind a broad reach becomes, the greater the amount of centerboard needed—usually just enough to aid in steering by keeping the craft from sliding to leeward of her course.

A broad reach is perhaps the easiest of all points of sailing, for there is not the worry over an unexpected jibe or the need for as lively, delicate balancing and **hiking** (action of crew placing their live weight on or beyond the boat's rail) as required with close reaching and windward sailing—although these factors must not be completely ignored. As a run or broad reach will take your boat to leeward and require beating back to her home base, practice in these points of sailing should be delayed until one has learned beam and close reaching, windward sailing, tacking, and jibing.

10. Practice Sailing

As soon as a skipper has a rudimentary knowledge of how to reach, run, and beat his boat to windward, and can execute the major maneuvers of tacking and jibing described in detail in foregoing chapters, he should turn his attention to increasing proficiency in sailing.

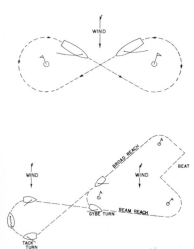

Left. A Jet 14 sloop on a beam reach, the point of sailing which beginners should practice first over a short course. (Courtesy, Siddons & Sindle) *Right.* A specified course with objectives is the best way to learn sailing. *Above*—a beam reaching course around marks (100 to 200 yards apart) to be turned by tacking is best for beginners. *Below*—a triangular course, with a third mark placed 100 yards or more to windward of the first, is the second step and provides beating, broad and beam reaching, tacking, and jibing (gybing) with the alternative of a tack at the second turn in strong winds.

In acquiring skill, a goal or object is needed, otherwise the tendency exists to take the easiest way out. This means choosing simply to reach back and forth across the wind and avoiding windward work or, if needed to reach a destination, struggling to weather most cautiously. By this approach, helmsmen sail timidly and will add little to their skill as skippers. Moreover, this very caution may lead to trouble by

73

Left. When practicing windward sailing, keep the hull nearly upright and meet the puffs by hiking, as Eric Olsen and crew demonstrate with Flying Dutchman Jr. (Courtesy, Geveke & Co.)
Right. When broad reaching, sails are slacked well off, as on this Gannett. (Courtesy, George D. O'Day Associates)

failing to give full control of their craft. In either case, they will not be respected by true sailors, most likely becoming the butt of the latters' jokes.

The best way to attain helmsmanship skill is by sailing a prescribed course which includes all points of sailing, tacking, and jibing. Even when learning to beam reach back and forth, a course with definite turning marks helps. Such courses can be laid out in a relatively small area, as the objective is frequent tacking, jibing, and adjusting of sails.

If existing navigational aids (buoys and stakes) are present, they will often provide a natural reaching or triangular course for practice. Mooring buoys or stakes in a cove, harbor, or river also can be utilized. If none of these is readily available, three short planks or small fireplace logs with holes bored in one end, old crab or lobster trap floats, or sealed five-gallon cans will serve. Attach lines of sufficient length for mooring with a small anchor, weight, or even a rock, then locate these buoys to form a reaching or triangular course.

The course can be laid out to accomplish both reaching and

74

triangular course practice. As beginners may need to practice reaching for a couple of days before attempting to sail a triangle, and winds usually do not blow from the same direction for prolonged periods, chances are that the buoys will have to be reset. The reaching course simply requires proceeding at right angles to the wind and dropping two buoys 100 to 200 yards apart. The new skipper sails back and forth, tacking around the buoy when he reaches either end of the course (see upper diagram of drawing on page 73).

The triangular course is set up by placing a third buoy roughly 200 yards directly to windward of the buoy marking the starting point of the reaching course. When sailing the course, the boat proceeds from the first mark to windward in two or more tacks, trying to reach her objective as quickly as possible. A skipper learns, among other things, when his boat can tack for a buoy in order to **fetch** (attain, lay, or reach a mark) without **overstanding,** or failing to fetch—that is, going too far or not far enough. A boat either can tack around the mark or bear off at the buoy onto the next course, depending on which tack the final approach is made. At the end of the second leg—a broad reach—a jibe will be necessary; then a close reach back to the starting point follows. If the wind is strong, a boat may tack at the second mark until the skipper has become proficient at jibing (see lower diagram of accompanying drawing). It is better to sail around a short course such as prescribed here, requiring the repeating of several maneuvers, than to go over a longer course demanding fewer actions. An interesting variation is to go around the triangle once; then, upon reaching the windward or first mark a second time, run directly back to the starting point and jibe around this mark before going over the triangle again.

In light winds with a boat of simple rig (such as a catboat), a new skipper often can practice single-handed rather than wait for an experienced sailor to spare the time to accompany him. After a little experience is gained, another novice may be shipped as crew, but two very inexperienced persons in a boat may only cause confusion.

Interest can be added to practice if other boats sail the short course at the same time. This will add competitive zest and point up errors, especially if skippers talk over what happened on the water upon going ashore or between brushes. When a more experienced skipper joins these practice sessions, ask him for instructive criticism.

While it is not the purpose of this book to discuss the fine points of racing nor the rules governing competitions, it should be pointed out that there is no better way to acquire small boat sailing skill than through competitive sailing. No one should be afraid to seek competition once the basic maneuvers of handling a boat have been acquired with a fair degree of proficiency. Engaging in formal sailboat racing, as distinct from informal brushes, will require a knowledge of yacht racing rules. These differ from the Rules of the Road, applying whenever two boats meet, to be discussed in the next chapter.

For beginners, the best competitive practice is to race over a short course against a single opponent. Right-of-way situations and racing strategy are less complicated in this type of competition, known as **match racing.** This is the form of competition used in the America's Cup races and provides a great deal of fun as well as being instructive, especially over a short course such as outlined here. Prior to participation in real racing, the beginner should ask an experienced skipper for instruction in racing rules and basic racing tactics.

It is well to avoid starting competitive sailing at the top. Some racing centers have only one class of boats and hence there is no choice, though there may be divisions based on age or experience. It is best to race against persons who are more experienced in order to learn. At the same time, to compete only against experts whose boats are halfway over the horizon before your craft can sail a quarter mile is apt to be discouraging, and the fun of sailing lost.

11. The Right of Way Rules

Waterways, whether oceans, lakes, rivers, or harbors, are highways of travel used by commercial and pleasure vessels; hence, traffic rules are needed. Although often marked by buoys to keep boats from going aground or astray, these water thoroughfares are not as clearly defined as highways. As they are infinitely broader than land roads, boats meet not only passing in the same or opposite direction, but crossing at angles almost anywhere. Well traveled waterways, therefore, can be one continuous intersection requiring a sharp lookout.

Left. **Why right-of-way rules are needed: Turnabouts meeting on different tacks and points of sailing. (Courtesy, National Turnabout Assn.)** *Right.* **Who's PRIVILEGED and who's BURDENED? Two Indian Class knockabouts meet. No. 96, the burdened boat on the port tack, must keep clear of No. 85 on starboard tack. (Photo by Clifton Feero)**

The regulations governing water traffic are called Rules of the Road, and are the basis upon which maritime law is interpreted. Rules of the Road cover all meetings, crossings, and convergings of vessels. They were designed primarily to avoid collisions, so they are written to make one vessel responsible for keeping clear of another. It is just as essential to know and observe the Rules of the Road when on the water as it is to know and observe traffic rules when driving a car.

A primary rule is that powerboats stay clear of, or yield right of way to, sailing craft—and both have to yield to boats

Left. The Sailfish, to windward, is burdened to stay clear of Sunfish, the leeward and privileged boat. (Courtesy, Alcort, Inc.) **Right.** Who's BURDENED and PRIVILEGED, here, when two Sprites meet? No. 4 has a double duty to keep clear, being both the boat on port tack and the one with the wind aft. (Courtesy, George D. O'Day Associates)

propelled by oars and paddles. The principal exception is that overtaking boats, regardless of motive power, keep clear of a craft which is being overtaken.

When sailboats meet, Article 17 of the Rules of the Road applies. These rules are not to be confused with sailboat racing rules, which differ considerably. Article 17 reads:

"ARTICLE 17. When two sailing vessels are approaching one another, so as to involve risk of collision, one of them shall keep out of the way of the other as follows, namely:

(a) A vessel which is running free shall keep out of the way of a vessel which is close-hauled.

(b) A vessel which is close-hauled on the port tack shall keep out of the way of a vessel which is close-hauled on the starboard tack.

(c) When both are running free, with the wind on different sides, the vessel which has the wind on the port side shall keep out of the way of the other.

(d) When both are running free, with the wind on the same side, the vessel which is to the windward shall keep out of the way of the vessel which is to the leeward.

(e) A vessel which has the wind aft shall keep out of the way of the other vessel." *

---

*International and Inland rules give nearly identical wording for Article 17, the difference being in sect. (d), where International Rules omit the article "the" before windward and leeward.

There also are certain rules of courtesy which should be observed whether or not they are spelled out in the Rules of the Road. The boat obligated to keep clear is known as the **burdened vessel** and the other craft as the **privileged vessel.** Therefore, a sailboat does not deliberately tack, sail a zig-zag course, or otherwise obstruct a burdened powerboat from keeping clear.

On the other hand, courtesy demands that powerboats give sailboats a reasonably wide berth, more than just enough to avoid collision, since their wake can shake wind from sails. In light airs this is extremely annoying, as sailboats require considerable time to regain previous momentum. Neither sailboats nor powerboats should be operated in a reckless or careless manner around floats or beaches where people are swimming.

From the above, skippers will realize the extreme importance of alertness and the necessity of maintaining a proper watch when sailing. Even a privileged vessel can be found equally guilty with a burdened vessel in courts or Coast Guard inquiries if her skipper did not maintain a proper lookout.

The basis of the Rules of the Road is the premise that a boat shall stay clear of situations involving the risk of collision. This means keeping well away from any danger. If collisions occur, skippers of burdened vessels have to do some tall explaining to the enforcing agency having jurisdiction. The sailboat skipper, provided he does not willfully operate his craft in close quarters, usually will be able to keep out of trouble if he obeys the few general rules and courtesies plus the five basic rules of Article 17 listed earlier.

These sailing rules were written largely in the days when most sailing craft were square-rigged. As these vessels maneuvered most easily when sailing free, the rules made ships which were sailing off the wind the burdened vessel, required to give way to a craft sailing close-hauled or to windward. For the purpose of this rule, any vessel not working to windward, that is, any craft with her sheets eased or pursuing a course other than to windward, is considered to be sailing free and therefore a burdened vessel.

When both vessels are close-hauled, the one on port tack is burdened and must keep clear of a starboard tack boat. Port tack again is burdened to keep clear when two craft are sailing free with the wind coming from different sides, hence sailing on different tacks. When boats are sailing free on the same tack, the boat to windward is burdened and must stay clear of, even if it means tacking away from, the leeward vessel. A sailing vessel having the wind aft is burdened to keep out of the way of another sailing vessel.

Another rule whereby an overtaking vessel is burdened has important aspects to bear in mind. When boats are converging, except sailboats meeting on opposite tacks, one vessel is always overtaking another regardless of whether sail or power craft are involved. Any craft approaching another on a course which lies anywhere between two compass points abaft the beam to directly astern of the leading vessel, is overtaking with the burden to stay clear. As sailboats rarely overtake powerboats, many skippers are unaware of their obligation to keep clear in this circumstance, which occasionally does happen.

When a collision occurs at sea or on an inland body of water, someone has violated the Rules of the Road, or safety rules which apply whenever boats are operating near craft, underway or at anchor.

Because different conditions exist, slightly varying rules are in force, depending upon the waters in which a boat is being operated. Suffice to say here that International Rules apply on the high seas beyond United States territorial waters; and Inland Rules are in force in coastal waters, on Lake Champlain, and most other bodies of water bordering on more than one state or nation.

The Great Lakes have their own definite rules, as do certain western rivers. Where lakes, ponds, and rivers are entirely within the boundaries of one state—Lakes Hopatcong in New Jersey, Winnipesaukee in New Hampshire, George in New York, and Mendota in Wisconsin are examples—the states prescribe special navigational rules, as these are not Federal waterways.

This chapter is concerned mainly with a few basic rules applying to sailing. If a person desires more information, there are worthwhile chapters in Charles F. Chapman's "Piloting, Seamanship, and Small Boat Handling," textbook for the excellent courses given by the United States Power Squadrons in the interest of boat safety.

Prior to racing, a skipper must learn the special rules evolved to govern the competitive situations where boats must be navigated in close quarters, in contrast to the Rules of the Road designed to avoid danger of collision. The racing rules of the North American Yacht Racing Union (1959 edition) govern all competitions except ocean racing, where the Rules of the Road apply, and copies may be obtained by writing that organization at 37 West 44th Street, New York City.

A DOZEN SAFETY RULES TO AVOID TROUBLE AFLOAT

For the sake of handy reference and greater emphasis, 12 MAJOR RULES OF SAFETY AFLOAT, dealt with in detail in Chapters 11–13, are listed below:

1. NEVER GO AFLOAT WITHOUT MAKING YOUR INTENTIONS KNOWN.
2. BE SURE YOUR BOAT IS PROPERLY EQUIPPED.
3. DON'T OVERLOAD A BOAT.
4. DON'T CLOWN—with or in boats!
5. OBEY RIGHT-OF-WAY RULES.
6. WATCH THE SKY FOR STORM CLOUDS AND WEATHER SIGNS!
7. NEVER CLEAT SHEETS in small boats.
8. DON'T GO OUT IN BOATS UNLESS YOU CAN SWIM (or are wearing a lifejacket). Learn Man Overboard Procedure.
9. STAY WITH A CAPSIZED OR SWAMPED BOAT.
10. KNOW YOUR WATERS.
11. KEEP BOAT ALWAYS UNDER FULL CONTROL.
12. DON'T PANIC.

12. Watch the Sky

Weather and its peculiarities are important to sailors. Sailboat skippers are primarily concerned with weather prospects and how these will affect their immediate plans. Their first source of information should be U.S. Weather Bureau and private forecasts given by newspapers, radio and television. Other indications may be gleaned from a variety of sources— a study of meteorology, the behavior of weather patterns in your area, and familiarity with the signs which nature provides, especially through watching the sky.

Left. Lakes surrounded by hills and intervening valleys are susceptible to puffs of squall strength, requiring alertness from crews even when winds are mild. Note the three thunderheads just beyond the leech of No. 6602's mainsail. (Courtesy, Lightning Class Assn.)
Right. Although the Lightning pictured is not in an actual squall, the craft would react similarly; she is heeled so far her hull and sails are losing their grip and a swamping is threatened. Hence the importance of shooting head-to-wind, to drop sails and anchor.
(Courtesy, Lightning Class Assn.)

Patterns and varieties of weather vary in different localities: Southern California, where thunder squalls are rare, has its "Santa Anas"; the Gulf of Mexico produces "northers"; San Francisco Bay and the Maine coast are noted for fogs; the South Atlantic coast is the area most prone to hurricanes; and New England is famous for northeasters.

There is good weather as well as bad, and it is the good

Left. Along the Atlantic seaboard, squalls often build or make up against light, cool sea breezes, whereas only a few miles inland warmer winds prevail and thunderheads rear skyward. (Morris Rosenfeld photo) *Right.* Calm before squall? Lightnings drift with little wind in 104° temperature as thunderheads commence to rise over the hill behind the Fort Worth Boat Club in Texas. (Courtesy, Lightning Class Assn.)

weather the sailor particularly seeks. Since even the most up-to-date radio-TV predictions are subject to change, the sailor—ever alert for development of unfavorable conditions— can and must use the sky as a bulletin board!

Discussion of the infinite variety of storms which appear over various points on the North American continent will not be undertaken here. However, each sailor must learn something of the weather apt to prevail or develop during the sailing season in his particular locality. A general rule requiring considerable interpretation and adaptation is that areas of low barometric pressure usually bring unfavorable weather, whereas high-pressure areas produce improving and normally clear weather. This book's aim is to help a sailor anticipate and meet weather conditions unfavorable to the enjoyment of his sport. Of these, squalls and fog provide the most general concern.

Squalls fall into several categories. The most awesome is the thunderstorm—brief, but mightily impressive and some-times vicious. A squall is any sudden burst of wind or, for that matter, rain or snow. Squalls may appear during light airs or calms, or in the midst of a gale. Often, they bring a change of wind direction. A squall, by its very name, implies stormy weather of brief duration.

Normally, the sky telegraphs a squall's approach, but occasionally one strikes with almost no warning from a virtually clear sky. Perhaps a small, fast moving cloud will be the only advance notice. The most famous of such rare squalls struck off Staten Island, July 20, 1876, to capsize the 150' schooner, *Mohawk*, at anchor with sails hoisted, bringing tragic consequences to the owner's family and guests caught below.

To one able to read the signs, usually there is ample visual warning. Because many ominous clouds fail to materialize into severe squalls, one may become careless when watchfulness is ever-demanded. When sailing on lakes surrounded by hills, for example, sudden puffs of squall strength may blow over the tops of hills or sweep down intervening valleys to strike the water for the first time very near your boat. A sharp lookout to windward may give a vital few seconds' warning.

Left. **Though the ominous black cloud may not prove serious, the youthful crew of a Cadet in England have wisely donned lifejackets. There is nothing "sissy" about this precaution which many crack racing classes and clubs are now requiring when squalls impend and strong winds blow. (Courtesy, George D. O'Day Associates)** *Right.* **Heavily clouded skies do not always spell squalls or strong surface winds, so while the skippers of the Highlander and Comet should remain watchful, there is probably little to fear in this sky. (Courtesy, Customflex, Inc.)**

When squalls strike with little or no warning, all a skipper can do is react with alertness, head up into the wind and slack sheets, get his crew to windward with alacrity, and douse or, if necessary, cast loose any light sails the boat may be carrying. If the squall is vicious, all sails should be lowered and furled. When a squall gives warning, a skipper is wise to prepare before it strikes, organizing his crew for emergencies and, if the signs are really ominous, lowering sail and anchoring as one would in the face of a severe thundersquall.

Thunderstorms can be the most tempestuous squalls the average sailor is apt to encounter. Fortunately, thundersqualls nearly always herald their approach by the formation of massive cumulus clouds on the horizon. These squalls contain dangerously high winds just frequently enough to make precautions imperative.

Because prevailing winds in the northern hemisphere tend to blow from west to east, our weather, whether good or bad, normally moves in roughly the same direction. This is true especially of thunderstorms, which are very often the advance-guard of a cold front or high pressure area. When thunder-heads start to push their massive, rugged outlines higher and higher into the western sky, the skipper, with eyes watching the west, should begin preparations. Local conditions and peculiarities, it should be remembered, may cause these storms to approach from somewhat different directions than west.

Thunderheads are built up by the rising of warm surface air. The storm frequently approaches against the prevailing surface breeze, although not necessarily from exactly the opposite direction. When the rising warm air reaches 25,000′ or higher, a first rate squall is apt to be born; the higher the warm air rises, the greater the storm's intensity. The ascending warm air gradually loses momentum, cools, and gains density. Now accompanied by rain, it plunges earthward as a squall, which may be terrifying.

Although a cold front may contain several squalls along its line of approach, thundersqualls as a rule are not more than a few miles in diameter. Their severest winds occur in an even narrower path and the duration of a squall, from the moment of its build-up until dissipation many miles away, is seldom more than three hours.

An hour or two after the first cumulus clouds build up—

the interval occasionally is shorter—the clouds under the thunderheads suddenly grow blacker. This means the squall is headed in the observer's direction. On some days thunderheads linger for hours in the west without any storms developing in the area. Earlier claps of thunder may have warned a skipper to head for home or shelter. Now, against the ebony sky, flashes of lightning are seen and perhaps ominous low clouds roll underneath the black sky. It is well if the skipper headed for shelter early, for an approaching thunderstorm usually kills the wind and a calm exists for a short period before the dark line of wind starts to move swiftly across the water.

Now the squall virtually has struck, and a small boat skipper should immediately head his craft into the wind, drop sails quickly, and anchor. In some waters, stakes and crab or lobster buoys can serve as emergency moorings. When a squall is about to hit a cove or harbor, skippers are advised to pick up the first vacant mooring or tie up to a boat or float, rather than attempt to reach more distant moorings of their own.

If a squall strikes before a boat can be anchored safely, lower sail and endeavor to run before the wind under bare poles. A jib sometimes can be carried; but in severe squalls this could be dangerous for the new sailor, who will be better off without any sail during the first gusts, which are usually the most violent. The nearness of shore may make running before the wind impracticable, but centerboard boats often can be run up on a soft shore or sandy beach to provide greater safety than might exist in riding out a storm.

A good rule to observe when a squall impends, especially if cockpits are small and waters are apt to become rough quickly, is for the skipper to require everyone to don a lifejacket.

Though a threatening squall on the water never is to be treated lightly, new or prospective sailors should not become panicky over thoughts of what a squall might do. The U.S. Weather Bureau statistics in Technical Paper No. 7 point out that less than 10% of the squalls striking boating areas have initial gusts exceeding 23-knot velocities, and only 3% contain winds greater than 30 knots.

This writer has noted that extremely vicious squalls rarely strike the same locality more often than once in every 5 to 10 years. More than one bad squall at the same place in any season is unusual. Some areas have almost no thundersqualls, while the Midwest, Gulf of Mexico, and parts of the Middle Atlantic Coast have a larger percentage of line squalls, brought on by fast-moving cold fronts, than other sections. These tend to be more severe than localized thunderstorms.

In the more vicious squalls, hail may accompany heavy rain and the wind may reach such velocities as to blow spume or spray off the tops of the waves, with visibility becoming extremely limited.

In addition to learning to read the sky, which can foretell changes of weather besides squalls, every sailor should read newspaper forecasts and study weather maps. These predict a general pattern for the area, but may not pinpoint local weather. They usually warn when conditions are ripe for thundersquall development. Such forecasts are prepared several hours ahead, and weather sometimes changes rapidly. Radio and television broadcasts provide up-to-date Weather Bureau and Coast Guard information and warnings, which should be followed to gain the latest information before going afloat. The rapid increase of boating in the past decade has resulted in the introduction of special boating forecasts by newspapers, radio, and TV.

Along some seacoasts and the Great Lakes, fog can be a great hazard. General conditions leading to fog can be predicted; but fixing its exact time of arrival is much more difficult, as it often settles in patches between clear areas. Where fogs are a possibility, no skipper should venture outside his harbor or cove in a boat not equipped with a foghorn and compass. When fog starts to roll in, a skipper immediately should take compass bearings to determine his position, direction of wind, and his course to home anchorage or destination.

Every sailor should know how to read, box, and take bearings with a compass. Once bearings are taken, it is advisable to head for home if the visibility becomes limited to a half-mile or less.

When the wind is fair this involves little difficulty, but if windward work is necessary a greater problem exists. Unless skippers are very certain of their location, numerous short tacks are better than long hitches to windward in foggy weather. If your destination or familiar landmarks fail to appear within a reasonable time, it may be smart to anchor and await a clearing or a passing boat able to lead the way on the right course. Above all in squall or fog, don't panic.

Old salts have many ancient sayings which purport to foretell weather and its behavior, including the intensity of a squall by whether the wind or rain arrives first. While many seem to have a certain basis of fact, meteorologists tell us most are not to be fully relied upon as true weather predictions. Hence, new skippers should be cautious of accepting these often-rhymed old saws until acquiring the experience necessary to judge their validity.

The skies, type of clouds, and visibility each contain signs at times of approaching weather changes which sailors can learn to read. These observations, coupled with knowledge of the general weather pattern over the country, can be translated into advantageous advance information regarding from which quarter the wind will blow, its probable strength, and whether its direction will shift.

Many sailors soon acquire at least a passing interest in meteorology—a fascinating subject quite worth pursuing, but beyond the scope of this book.

13. Safety Afloat

Sailing is a splendid recreation—the safest of all water sports, with serious accidents rare.

Any form of boating can be very safe if proper precautions are taken; but with sailing, the wind provides a means of propulsion free from mechanical failure and danger from fire or explosion. Moreover, human strength is a less-decisive factor than in canoes or rowboats, permitting sailing to be enjoyed by many physically handicapped persons.

Left. **A transparent window in sail is an added safety feature, permitting crew to look to leeward while hiking as this Comet sails near a club—often a good place from which to maintain a watch on small boat and junior sailing.** *Right.* **The oar in this Quahog Dinghy, engaged in "Frost-bite" sailing, rates high on the list of safety MUSTS along with lifejackets, painter, and bailing equipment.**
(Courtesy, Casco Bay Boats)

Boating's tragedies and near-tragedies stem mainly from foolhardiness or inexperience, with lives lost, injuries sustained, or harrowing experiences undergone because the principles of safety afloat are violated. Accidents can and do happen in all types of pleasure craft when novices fail to learn, or excessively self-confident veterans believing in their own impunity, violate the rules of safe boating. Accidents can occur despite foresight and preparedness, but observance of simple rules will prevent most.

If sailing were 100% safe, a sizeable measure of its appeal would, as with most sports, be lost. The excitement comes from the unexpected challenge to a skipper's ability and resourcefulness.

True sailors show a healthy respect for the latent power of the elements controlled by Old Mother Nature, who usually warns of the intention to release her furies. The warning is not always sufficient, so the good sailor must always be alert. Every skipper, whether a novice in his first boat or an old hand with 50 years experience, should carefully observe the following **basic rules of safety** founded on common sense, experience, and the discouragement of foolhardiness.

NEVER GO AFLOAT WITHOUT MAKING YOUR INTENTIONS KNOWN. This first safety rule, especially applicable to novices, should be followed by all. A skipper ought to inform someone regarding his sailing plans (waters or destination), ask that a watchful eye be kept on his boat, and request a powerboat be sent out if bad weather threatens or the boat fails to return on schedule.

Wherever small boats manned by children or novices are sailing, an imperative procedure is to establish a regular watch,

Left. Modern molded fiberglass hulls have built-in flotation through airtight compartments forward and in stern, as in this Sprite. (Crossley photo, courtesy George D. O'Day Associates) **Right.** Open keel boats can also have built-in flotation, as witness this Hodgdon Brothers 21′ sloop—filled with water—supporting the added weight (375 lbs.) of two grown men.

Left. Eric Olsen demonstrates overloading in a Flying Dutchman Jr. Skipper is wedged behind tiller at transom; low freeboard, dragging stern, and cramped crew conditions could lead to trouble if the boat were in less experienced hands. (Courtesy, Geveke & Co.) *Right.* While perhaps not overloaded, procedures not recommended for safety afloat are demonstrated on this Sprite with a crewman sitting forward of the mast in a dinghy and skipper's position denying free movement of tiller. (Courtesy, George D. O'Day Associates)

kept either by private individuals or in conjunction with civic, scholastic, and yacht club training programs. The sailing area should be scanned constantly, with a frequent count of sails made in order to spot any craft in trouble and quickly send assistance. It is advisable for novices to sail only within sight of watchers and in well-frequented waters, where there is safety in numbers and hence less chance of a serious accident when capsizings or other troubles occur. The sailing fraternity has long lived by the old law of the sea calling for immediate succor of fellow sailors in trouble.

BE SURE YOUR BOAT IS PROPERLY EQUIPPED. This rule has many facets, the foremost being: there must be a life preserver, preferably a life jacket, for every person on board. A bailing scoop, bucket, and usually a pump are standard equipment. Even though pumped and sponged dry before a sail starts, no boat is immune to the sudden knock-down which may threaten a swamping. As a boat's maneuverability is greatly reduced when she is partially filled with water, a crew will need the means to bail fast in ridding her of perhaps barrels of unwanted water.

Another must is a good strong painter or tow rope. Nothing is more frustrating to a powerboat skipper, engaged in a rescue operation or an act of kindness when the wind fails, than to have the tow line break as soon as strain is placed upon it. Boat owners should discard lines showing signs of wear and make certain towing lines have adequate length.

Left. **This may not be intentional clowning, but the skipper of a Rhodes Bantam risks dunking his small daughter when he sails from the leeward side, where sudden puffs cannot be seen, with only an inch or two of freeboard. (Courtesy, Gibbs Boat Co.)** *Right.* **A life ring handy! It's always a good rule to have a life preserver, jacket, or ring almost within arm's reach, for crew members do fall overboard, whether one sails a cruising sloop of the pictured New Horizons Class or a dinghy. (Courtesy, Ray Greene & Co.)**

Every boat should be equipped with an anchor and rode, paddle or oars; no excuse exists for the lack of such equipment on any craft with foredeck, cuddy, or lazarette. Some contend anchors are bothersome in open or dinghy-type boats. When these craft are sailing close to shore with patrol boats operating or a watch posted, an anchor, though not paddles and painters, may be omitted. When a squall strikes, there is not always time to return to float or mooring, so before the real blow

Left. A capsized boat makes a good life raft, usually staying afloat with mast and sail resting on the water. Some boats may be righted as the crew of this Firefly is attempting during a race off Marblehead, Mass., thus allowing Lightnings to continue their race. (Courtesy, Mary Hogan) *Right.* Aids to navigation, such as this red-and-black lighted buoy marking a channel obstruction, may also serve as racing marks. This buoy is being rounded by Cirrus, a Thistle owned by Donald Kent, famed Boston radio-TV meteorologist whose prognostications have made him known the length of the New England Coast as "the yachtsman's friend." (Photo, courtesy of Clifton Feero)

starts, skippers should head craft into the wind, drop sails, and anchor. This prevents a boat from capsizing or being blown far off course, thus expediting rescue efforts and alleviating the worry of family and friends ashore.

A well-equipped boat has sound gear and rigging. An owner has the responsibility for checking the condition of hull, spars, and equipment frequently, as a protection both of his investment and for the safety of skipper and crew. Running rigging should run freely with ropes and wire able to withstand any sudden strain. Standing rigging must be checked frequently for serious corrosion and metal fatigue. A **parted** (broken) sheet or halyard could leave a boat helpless at the wrong moment, or rot in spars or rigging lead to dismasting. Sails in need of repair or replacement likewise can spell trouble in an emergency, and maintenance of hull against deterioration from the elements is equally important.

An added safeguard is proper flotation—accomplished by means of bulkheads, air tanks, special buoyant plastics, sponsons, or inflated heavy rubber tubes which provide built-in flotation at relatively small expense. Where fog is prevalent, a good compass and fog horn are required equipment.

DON'T OVERLOAD. Crowding or excess weight in a sailboat is dangerous. No craft should be undermanned; but overloading invites trouble, as nearly all boats are designed to sail their best when carrying weights within certain minimum and maximum limits. When these limits are exceeded a boat's maneuverability is taxed.

While designer and builder provide for some flexibility in size and weight of normal crew, if 5 persons are put in a boat designed to sail with 2 or 3, the craft will not be sailing on her intended lines. By displacing more water, she requires greater ·power to drive and hence becomes sluggish. A boat needs all possible maneuverability when called upon to react to the unexpected puff or any emergency.

In sailing dinghies, 2 persons are a usual crew, with any more than 3 overcrowding. With other small centerboarders, a great deal depends on the size of the cockpit. Snipes and Comets, with small cockpits, can safely carry just about the same number as dinghies. Craft with larger cockpits may take 3 with ease, sometimes 4, or perhaps 5 without overloading.

Dangers from excess weight and overcrowding, apparent to experienced sailors, may not always be realized by the uninitiated. In puffs, when sailing in close quarters, or during emergencies, skipper and crew must be able to work their boat without hindrance. If required to climb over or push aside other people in order to reach vital gear, the delay could cause an accident. In most small boats and dinghies, overloading reduces freeboard dangerously. When the breeze increases suddenly or the boat rounds a point to enter rougher water, excess weight can bring trouble, maybe disaster.

DON'T CLOWN. This phrase, subject of posters in the Coast Guard's campaign during National Safe Boating Week each summer, points to the fact that many accidents are caused by foolhardy, show-off actions of immature "boatsteerers," unworthy to be honored with the title "Skipper." The danger may be greater when power craft are involved, but clowning at the helm of sailboats also is dangerous.

A miscalculation when trying to scare occupants of another boat might result in one craft climbing aboard or staving a hole in the other. A skipper may have utmost confidence in

his ability to maneuver in close quarters, but the other helmsman, not knowing his intentions, may become excited and alter helm at just the wrong moment. A collision or perhaps the overturning of one boat results. Collisions even of small boats have caused severe lacerations or broken bones to occupants. A young man of the writer's acquaintance once was appalled when the exploding of a Fourth of July cherry bomb, which he tossed under the bow of a friend's Two-Ten, resulted in the rapid sinking of this $2500 craft.

Fooling among the crew aboard one's own boat also can be risky. Playful shoving may cause injury to an unprepared

RIGHT AND WRONG for dinghy skippers is demonstrated by Stuart Allbright, a college sailing star when at Dartmouth, in one of the boats at Boston's Community Sailing Program. Note at left how a poor leeward position cramps movements of body and tiller. Seated to windward, right, skipper is free to watch sail, feel wind on face, handle sheets easily, and move quickly. (Courtesy, Jack Wood)

crew member falling overboard or against a hard object. A crack on the head from the boat's side or boom might bring loss of consciousness and a drowning. Such accidents, fortunately, are rare, but the beginner is cautioned against attitudes other than alertness toward safety when sailing. While sailing is and always should be fun, one must never forget that consequences of the unexpected act can be serious.

NEVER CLEAT YOUR SHEETS. When sailing any centerboard boat or keel craft lacking a watertight or self-bailing cockpit, sheets must never be cleated—PARTICULARLY THE MAINSHEET—as a knockdown can swamp such craft very quickly. The mainsheets on these boats always should be held directly or snubbed around a winch or jam cleat. Thus held by skipper or crew, the sheet is ready to be let out instantly when need arises. When the wind has such strength that the sheet will slip from one's grip if not so caught (snubbed), the single turn on the winch or jam cleat can be freed quickly.

The slip hitch (a form of half-hitch where a loop instead of an end is caught under the last turn on a cleat) is especially recommended for use on moderate-size keel sailboats where the pull of mainsheet may be too great for an individual to handle. This slip hitch is excellent for halyards on all small boats, offering a quick method of releasing cleated rope when necessary.

DON'T GO OUT IN BOATS UNLESS YOU CAN SWIM. Persons unable to swim at least 25 to 50 yards should never go or be taken in sailboats unless willing to wear a lifejacket at all times. Even experienced sailors occasionally slip overboard.

If a crew member falls overboard without a lifejacket, immediately throw him a line, lifejacket or preserver, cushion, oar, or floorboard—anything to which a man overboard may cling and which marks the spot of the mishap. Then organize your craft so a proper jibe may be executed. Hasty jibing may do more damage than good, perhaps carrying away gear or swamping the boat.

Once jibed, the boat should be headed back along roughly the course she was sailing. A jibe is used because the boat's approach should be slightly to leeward of the spot where the crew fell overboard. This advantage will be lost if the boat is tacked, but when a craft is short-handed in strong winds the skipper should consider tacking rather than risk damage from a poorly executed jibe.

When the man overboard is spotted, take care to edge the boat up to a point where, when shot into the wind, she will come alongside the person easily and with only moderate way. Under-or over-shooting may require a second try when time is vital. With a boat head-to-wind, a person usually can be hauled over the windward rail into the cockpit. A strong sailor may help himself aboard, provided he has not been in the water too long. A length of line with a loop large enough to slip over a man's shoulders will aid in bringing a person alongside and on board. Hauling a man over the transom rarely is advised, for small boats normally will not stay head-to-wind for long, and this method often interferes with full use of tiller.

STAY WITH YOUR BOAT IF YOU SWAMP OR CAPSIZE. This is a cardinal rule of boat safety! Each summer the newspapers report drownings when boats swamp or capsize. Almost invariably the story relates how the helpless, poor swimmer remaining with the boat was rescued, while a strong swimmer, who decided to strike out for shore and help, failed to reach his destination.

The chances are strong an overturned boat will eventually be spotted either from shore, air, or passing craft. An hour or more may elapse, it is true, before rescue is effected, but the odds favor survival of people who stick by their boat, either by hanging on from the water or climbing on the overturned hull. Any man who swims for shore, after the exertions occurring when a boat swamps, risks losing his life from cold water exposure or fatigue.

Remember, also, life is more vital than any boat's equipment. When no rescue is in sight, conserve energy. Don't swim around trying to save sails or floating gear. These can wait until rescue craft arrive. Even then, it is better to let a fresh person go overboard to salvage gear, or lose it altogether. Sailors have drowned within a few feet of rescue craft, simply because fatigue or cramp from exposure suddenly overtook them.

The words "capsize," "swamp," and "overturn" often have frightening overtones for persons who have never experienced such accidents. Capsizing, of itself, almost never is dangerous. The aftermaths or consequences of capsizing are what cause trouble.

In fact, this writer believes no sailor can become a qualified skipper until he experiences a capsizing. If one has never capsized, a haunting fear often exists and a skipper sails overcautiously; or, in the belief that only the inexperienced or inept capsize, another type of skipper takes foolish risks. Few things are better than a capsizing to alleviate the fear of suddenly being thrown into the water and to teach how a boat behaves. Many skippers have capsized without getting wet above the knees.

When a centerboard boat capsizes, she usually rolls slowly over on her side and will rest with mast and sail on the water for some time. There are circumstances, most likely to occur during righting efforts, when a craft will "turn turtle." A few centerboard boats, carrying inside ballast without the safeguard of adequate flotation, may sink. This is true, of course, when a heavily ballasted keel craft, without watertight cockpit or special flotation, suffers a knockdown and swamps. A boat is said to swamp when she fills with water without turning on her side or over; but unless she can be bailed out speedily and her sails lowered, the danger of capsizing or sinking is imminent.

Many small sailboats today are designed so that, after capsizing, they can be righted by the crew without outside assistance. In certain racing classes it is common to see the crew right the boat (usually by standing on the centerboard), climb aboard, bail out, continue, and even win the race.

As a rule, small sailboats will float to provide a raft which may be occupied or clung to for several hours after capsizing. Hence, capsizing, instead of rating as a calamity, is rather a necessary lesson in how to handle a boat properly. Moreover, a line should be drawn—perhaps fine, but distinct—between always obeying the rules of safe boating and overdoing the safe-boat idea. Skippers who learn to sail in reasonably lively capsizeable boats have far better chances of becoming good helmsmen and real seamen than those who venture out only in ultra-safe, usually under-rigged, sailboats—and perhaps then only in light winds.

KNOW YOUR WATERS. **Charts** (nautical maps) are available for all Federal waters and for some larger lakes within state boundaries. Study of charts, supplemented by keen observation afloat, will show the location of rocks and shoals where unwary skippers might run craft aground with consequences ranging from inconvenience to considerable damage. By showing varying depths and location of channels, charts can explain the pattern of local tides or currents—factors that may speed or delay arrival at a destination or possibly carry a boat into real danger. Finally, charts show the location of aids to navigation, why they are placed in that position, and whether they transmit audible or visual signals to assist a skipper in thick weather, fog, or after dark.

For smaller lakes and ponds, skippers must rely mainly on what is termed "local knowledge." Novices should talk to older boatmen, who normally are eager to display their knowledge and familiarity with the body of water. Old salts on any waterfront generally are willing to aid a new if respectful sailor with a desire to learn, even though they may engage in a bit of leg-pulling or tall-yarn spinning in the bargain. Knowledge of sailing waters will do more than keep your boat out of trouble; it will make you a better sailor and seaman.

ALWAYS KEEP A BOAT UNDER FULL CONTROL. This rule simply reiterates under one heading previous comments on the importance of having a sailboat under full control (when sufficient wind for steerageway exists) to provide proper maneuverability. The necessity of keeping the sails full enough to provide the momentum required for tacking has been stressed, and the fact noted that under-rigged boats are sluggish, responding slowly to the helm. Carrying too much sail likewise can cause a skipper to lose control of a sailboat. The boat may tip so much she tends to wallow rather than progress normally through the waves; or, she may luff, or broach sharply into the wind with little or no warning. Either spells real trouble.

DON'T PANIC. This last rule means exactly what it says: remain calm when faced with the unexpected. Panic often results in either making the wrong decision, or the lack of any decision—and that is usually worse than the emergency itself! Prompt reactions are needed on boats, but weighing the consequences is equally vital. Certain tensions are bound to arise on boats where quick actions are important. However fashionable, traditional, or natural it may seem to new skippers to cuss and scream, being a Captain Bligh rarely is conducive to efficient boat handling. It may frighten the wits out of a not-too-experienced crew, leading to panic.

14. Basic Knots

A thorough knowledge of marlinspike seamanship—which includes uses of rope, many knots, hitches and bends, whipping, seizing and splicing—traditionally has been required before new sailors were allowed to venture far afloat. Since the average skipper rarely uses more than a few knots, it is better to master the tying and usage of a half-dozen good ones than to learn many fancy knots not vitally needed. Granted an anchor bend is the preferred method of securing rode to anchor, nevertheless a bowline will permit the new sailor to get by with reasonable safety.

Left. **Rope coiled and hung from cleat on top of the cuddy in a popular Day Sailer sloop, one of the newest fiberglass family boats. (Courtesy, George D. O'Day Associates)** *Right.* **A bosun at the M.I.T. Nautical Association shows the proper way to heave a line with an underhand swing and toss. Note how one end of line is held under the left foot to prevent uncleated line from being lost overboard as it pays out.**

Synthetic ropes of nylon or Dacron have largely displaced traditional manila and the fine Italian hemp ropes so much admired for yachts 20 years ago. Manila still is serviceable, though its harsh feel and splintered ends are hard on hands, making softer lines preferred on small boats, even when more expensive. Synthetic ropes do not mildew and rot, outlasting manila and hemp for sheets subjected to constant

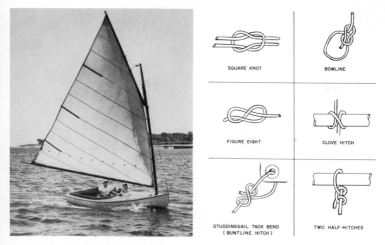

SQUARE KNOT

BOWLINE

FIGURE EIGHT

CLOVE HITCH

STUDDINGSAIL TACK BEND
(BUNTLINE HITCH)

TWO HALF-HITCHES

Left. The square knot's second name is reef knot, because it is used to tie together the reef points, shown on the sail of this Beetle Cat. Reefing shortens sail by securing a small portion of the sail furled along the boom, but very few modern racing sails have reef points. (Courtesy, Concordia Co., Inc.) *Right.* A collection of six important knots, ample for permitting new skippers to go afloat safely.

wetness. Since synthetics often last several seasons, they are more economical than ropes of natural fiber requiring frequent replacement.

When using synthetic rope, remember that nylon stretches more easily than Dacron fibers, hence nylon is recommended where elasticity is advisable, such as for a mooring line. Dacron is preferred for halyards and guys where stretch is undesirable. Synthetic ropes are stronger, with ½″ diameter nylon having a minimum tensile strength of 4950 lbs., to Dacron 4500 and manila 2900. In weight, nylon and manila are almost equal, Dacron being about 2 lbs. heavier per 100′.

Modern rope for boats is twisted or braided. As most youngsters learned in Boy Scout manuals: "In a twisted rope, a few fibers are twisted to the right to form a yarn, then, a few yarns are twisted to the left to form a strand. Three strands are twisted to the right to form a rope, and three ropes twisted to the left form a cable-laid rope." The twist, called lay, can be ascertained by holding a rope up and down noting whether the threads, strands, or ropes slant upward to the right or left.

By alternating directions of twist, the fibers and strands pull against each other to make hard, compact rope capable of repelling water, withstanding heavy strain, and overcoming tendencies to untwist or fray. Marline, a two-threaded and left-handed strand, and other small line, will be found most handy on board any craft.

Braided line, extensively used on boats for main- and jibsheets, is advertised by cordage companies as superior to laid rope, as it does not kink or unlay, is soft and exceptionally strong.

The end of a piece of rope is the part that usually ties a knot, and may be called either the end or the **fall**. The **standing part** is the portion of the line between the ends. A **bight** is a more or less pronounced curve in a rope, which becomes a loop when the parts meet or cross. All sailors should be warned that a serious accident may result if an arm or leg is caught in a bight of rope upon which strain is placed.

Learning to coil rope and to heave a line properly is important. The landsman's fashion of coiling rope over elbow and between thumb and forefinger will bring hoots of derision from sailors. It should be remembered that coiling a secured rope is started near the end where it is fastened, because each loop makes a twist in the rope and this kink uncurls from the coil as the end is reached.

Nautical procedure calls for picking up the rope in the left hand, a foot or so from where secured or from an end. Next, the rope is grasped with right hand two or more feet farther on (size of desired coil governs) and brought around in a clockwise loop to the left hand; repeat the operation until the rope is properly coiled. If figure eight loops form due to stiffness, it will be necessary to twist the rope clockwise with the right hand as the rope is laid in the left.

Coiling a stiff rubber or plastic garden hose as prescribed above offers a good lesson in behavior of rope while being coiled. Left-handed rope should be coiled counter-clockwise. When a finished coil is to be hung on a cleat to which a portion of rope has been secured, reach through the coil, grasp the rope falling from the cleat, and bring this loop through the coil; after twisting twice, hang the loop over the horn or horns of the cleat.

Ability to heave a line properly to another boat, a man

overboard, or onto a pier is very necessary to expedite towing, rescuing, or landing. First, one end of the line is secured and the free rope is coiled in the left hand. Next, the number of coils necessary to reach the objective are shifted to the right hand and grasped tightly. The remaining coil is held lightly with the left to permit running free when the time comes.

To heave, the right hand is swung back and forth prior to tossing the coil underhanded, with the grip released just as the hand reaches its maximum forward swing. As this line goes out full length, permit the coil in the left to pay out as needed.

When a boat is about to be towed, however, remember to haul in any slack until the powerboat moves forward. Then, with a full turn around a cleat or bitt, the necessary length of towline is paid out slowly. This prevents loose rope fouling a propeller and allows the boat to gather speed gradually, avoiding a violent snap which might break the towline.

A half-dozen basic knots will give the new sailor the working repertoire pictured herein. Others can be learned as needed. Knots in the broad sense include bends and hitches as well; and, in the strict sense, are divided into binding knots which tie objects snugly together, and loop knots which hold objects when security comes first. Knots may be tied with the end or a bight of rope. **Hitches** tie ropes to or around objects for speedy, usually temporary, fastening. **Bends** join ropes together. There are occasional circumstances when all may be used for other purposes than the definitions state.

A few other terms may help in tying the six basic knots illustrated, with a few of their variations. An overhand loop crosses the end over the standing part; in an underhand loop the end crosses under. A turn is taken by looping a rope around an object, often another section of the rope. A round turn loops the rope twice around.

Square or Reef Knot: Among the knots most used by sailors, the square knot ranks with the tightest. But it does have three faults: working poorly with ropes of different sizes, jamming under tension or when wet, and untying when a free end is jerked. It ties up bundles, and when tied with loops becomes a bow knot used to tie shoe lacings.

To tie a square knot, take an end in each hand. Then pass the end held in the left hand over and under the right end.

Curve the new left end toward the right. The right end is now crossed over and under the left and the knot drawn tight. Note the square knot has two parts lying together under one loop and over the other, while the two ends emerge at the top with the standing parts below. A **granny,** which both slips and jams, results if the emerging parts straddle the loops. To tie two ropes together, even of unequal diameters, the **sheet bend,** or weaver's knot, is recommended. This is started by first making an overhand loop with an end of one rope. Next, pass the other end through this loop, up behind the standing part of the first rope and down again through the loop. This bend can be tied by first making a square knot, then retrieving one end from its loop and passing this end under its standing part but over its loop.

Half Hitch: Rarely used alone, this hitch provides the basic element for tying many knots. The end is passed around the object and an overhand knot tied to the standing part by pulling the end between the turn and the object. The hitch is strengthened if the end is nipped under the turn some distance from the standing part. Half hitches are used also to finish off cleating a rope by reversing the final turn so the end jams under the loop. This has a serious disadvantage when ropes need fast uncleating. A **slip,** or **slippery hitch,** where a bight rather than an end is looped under the standing part, is strongly recommended.

Two Half Hitches: This excellent method of securing rope to rings or other objects is made, as implied, by tying first one and then another half hitch. It does not matter whether the two hitches are passed around the standing part in the same direction, as shown in the illustration, or in opposite directions.

Clove Hitch: This valuable knot is a form of two half hitches. Its main nautical use is to secure lines to spars or the tops of pilings on piers. The easiest method is to toss two half hitches twisted the same way over the stake. This is accomplished by a flick of the wrist to the right to form underhand loops when thrown over the piling. When a rope cannot be tossed, make two underhand loops around the spar or object and tighten by pulling on both end and standing part. A clove's security may be increased by half-hitching the end to the standing part.

Buntline Hitch: This knot is tied in the same fashion as a four-in-hand necktie. In a variation called **topsail sheet** or **studdingsail tack bend,** the second half hitch is formed in the opposite direction so that the end passes under and then over the loop before being brought out under the first half hitch. These are good knots for securing sails to halyards and similar purposes, as pressure tends to tighten the knots.

Bowline: This is the sailor's knot often described as the king of knots, for it has many variations and uses, and never jams or slips. It will fasten an anchor to its rode, join two lines together, secure a boat to a ring bolt, serve as a sling to hoist a man or article aloft, or make a form of lasso.

To tie, an overhand loop is formed and held in place with the fore and middle fingers of the right hand on top, and the thumb underneath with the third finger alongside to guide the making of a second loop. The left hand holds the bight between thumb and index finger. Next, the right hand is turned palm up, to form a loop through which the end leads upward. The left hand catches and holds this loop at the intersection almost automatically. The end is now passed by the right hand under and over the standing part and finally back through the small loop to complete the bowline.

The **running bowline** forms a noose, a **bowline on a bight** can make a useful loop in the middle of a rope, and a **double bowline** is excellent for a sling.

Figure Eight: This symmetrical knot has a limited usage—principally as a stopper to prevent the end of a rope unreeving through a block or fairlead. It is tied by forming an overhand loop, then passing the end under the standing part and back, over and under, through the loop. It can be tied also as an overhand knot with a twist made at the top of the loop before the end is led through.

Eventually, skippers should learn to splice rope, a simple operation which can be picked up along with tying other knots by consulting Boy and Sea Scout manuals. There are several fine books on the subject by Cyrus L. Day, Clifford Ashley, and George Russell Shaw, or Geumont and Hensel's *Encyclopedia of Knots and Fancy Rope Work,* which list more than 100 different means of securing and uniting ropes. With the advent of synthetic rope, whipping the ends is done largely by mechanical and chemical binding processes to prevent fraying and raveling, but remains a useful accomplishment. *105*

15. Selecting Your Boat

Buying a boat is always an adventure, but never more exciting than when a new sailor is acquiring his first craft. It is intriguing to go to boat shows, visit showrooms, prowl about boatyards, and travel the countryside to look over craft stored in back yards, garages, or boat sheds, in order to find just the right boat.

Left. The Rebel, a 16′ centerboard sloop with good lines and ample sail area to perform in localities where breezes range from light to moderate. (Courtesy, Ray Greene & Co.) *Right.* A Bullseye, fiberglass version of the famed keel 12½-footers which the late Nathanael G. Herreshoff, Wizard of Bristol, designed for the youngsters sailing the windy, rugged waters of Buzzards and Narragansett Bays. (Courtesy, Cape Cod Shipbuilding Co.)

The prospective buyer will need advice from experienced sailors. Moreover, he should be prepared for some conflicting opinions, because every "expert" possesses his own ideas on the merits of different types of sailboats. The veteran yachtsman will be able, nevertheless, to give valuable opinions concerning construction, seaworthiness, rig, equipment, cost and, in the case of a second-hand boat, whether the craft is a good buy.

Whether to purchase a catboat or sloop, keel or centerboard yacht, chine or round-bottomed craft, or wooden or fiberglass

Left. The Mercury, a 15′ sloop with moderate rig and comparatively high freeboard, which can be purchased either with keel or centerboard. (Courtesy, Cape Cod Shipbuilding Co.) *Right.* The International Star, first of the great one-design classes which spread throughout the world, is still constructed as a planked wooden boat as are many Lightnings and Snipes. Once called the "poor man's racing yacht," this sloop requiring delicate tuning retains her popularity despite expense and lack of a spinnaker. (Morris Rosenfeld photo)

boat—this becomes the final decision of the purchaser after listening to experts and weighing all opinions.

Any author approaches the subject of selecting a boat with some apprehensions. The intention is to help sailors make a decision by pointing out features desirable in both first and later boats, rather than to say a Snipe, Blue Jay, Herreshoff 12-footer, or a racing dinghy is the best boat. Being a yachtsman, and human, the writer cannot refrain from expressing at times his positive opinions about small boats.

The ideal sailboat, for beginner or expert, has yet to be designed. Although many men have tried, it may never be achieved. Nearly all popular sailboats marketed in the United States and Canada have good points, and most have at least one weakness. Almost all craft built today in the small boat classification are designed to race, but some class boats are distinctly more sporty than others.

The selection of the boat best suited to the new owner

requires consideration of the cost of purchasing, equipping, and maintaining, plus the local water and weather conditions. Such interrelation of all points exists that, while they can be discussed separately, they may not be divorced in reaching conclusions.

What Type Boat?

Prevailing weather conditions at a locality where the boat will be sailed provide an important part of the answer. The ideal craft for Newport Harbor or Puget Sound on the West Coast, and Long Island Sound or Marblehead on the Atlantic seaboard, where light to moderate winds and comparatively deep water prevail, will not necessarily be as suitable for San Francisco and Buzzards Bays, where strong winds and rough waters are the rule. The comparatively shallow waters of Lakes St. Clair and Erie produce a different type of sea than is found on far-deeper Lakes Michigan and Ontario, where a sailor, except for the absence of salt in the spray, might imagine he was sailing the Atlantic or Pacific.

Certain boats will react differently than others to each set of conditions. Barnegat and Great South Bays are so shallow

Left. The Bantam, a grown-up sloop version of the Penguin Dinghy, is a speedy, roomy, but not-too-extreme craft; especially popular in smooth waters, it may be home-built of plywood. (Courtesy, Gibbs Boat Co.) *Right.* A race of the Nipper Class, one of several popular catboat classes which include Beetles, Nippers, Woodpussies, Snowbirds, Moths, and Hustlers. (Courtesy, Ray Greene & Co.)

as to virtually demand a centerboard boat despite their strong breezes, whereas many keel craft sail on Chesapeake Bay and Lake Ponchartrain, even though they do not possess as deep water as the Maine coast or Lake Huron.

Centerboard Boats: This writer holds the opinion, seconded by many crack skippers, that centerboard boats are the best craft in which to learn to sail. Unless under-rigged, the centerboarder usually is livelier than her keel sister, requiring alertness on the part of crew and skipper. Such a craft, as noted in earlier chapters, best teaches the importance of

Left. A simple boat of catamaran design, the Gunderdink is exceptionally light weight—only 98 pounds—and carries a 35 square foot mainsail and optional jib. (Courtesy, Gunderson Catamaran Co.) *Right.* The 10′ Vixen, a moderate dinghy, comes in both sloop and cat rigged versions to make a good trainer. (Courtesy, Ray Greene & Co.)

sailing boats on their feet, or designed lines, without exaggerated angles of heel. If a centerboard boat capsizes, she normally provides a good life raft.

Centerboard boats are able to sail in shallower waters than keel craft, usually drawing less water and, more important, their boards may be raised if a shoal is encountered. As a rule the cost of centerboard boats, new or second-hand, is lower, and maintenance factors also tend to reduce expenses. One of the best arguments for the centerboard boat is the fact that

Left. **The Trident carries a sliding gunter, rather than the lug or lateen, rig of some sailing surfboards, making, with hinged rudder and centerboard, for easy maneuverability. (Courtesy, Merriman Bros.)** *Right.* **The famed Optimist Class pram, sponsored by the Optimist Clubs for junior sailing programs in which thousands of youngsters have learned to become good sailors despite the box-like hulls and the cumbersome-appearing sprit rig. (Woody Thayer photo, courtesy Pat Mason)**

a high percentage of this nation's ranking skippers, including men who have gone on to race keel boats in top-flight competition, had early training in centerboard craft that taught the importance of balance and to keep the boat sailing nearly upright when on the wind.

Keel Boats: The adherents of the keel boat are apt to center their case around two points. One is the safety factor, which has some justification where winds are strong and seas rough, for there is no safer, abler boat than a well-designed keel craft equipped with built-in flotation or a watertight, self-bailing cockpit. The other point, heard less often in these days of rising costs, is that if one lives in a deep water area where keel boats predominate, sailors might as well commence by learning to sail this type. If accepted, one must be prepared for greater expense and even some restriction of mobility, both ashore and afloat.

Design: Until nearly three decades ago, small sailboats were designed largely to fit the conditions encountered at one port, or perhaps a few neighboring harbors. Starting with the famous Star Class, a trend developed to design small boats able to perform reasonably well and engage in championship competitions in many far-flung localities. No boat has yet been designed which will sail as well and be equally popular in light breezes and smooth seas as in strong winds and rough waters. Even the world-girdling Stars with their large sail area are more suited to Long Island Sound than to San Francisco Bay. This is true in varying degrees of Lightnings, Snipes, Comets, Blue Jays, and all popular one-designs, but an owner may still obtain a great deal of sport with a Star in the strong sou'westers of Narragansett Bay, or fun with a Bullseye in the summer breezes of Massachusetts Bay or the Chesapeake.

Beginners, however, may not want a boat in which one gets thoroughly soaked and needs to be acrobatic at hiking whenever the wind goes above 10 **knots** (nautical miles per hour). They should steer clear of over-canvassed racing machines, but will neither learn fast nor well in heavy displacement, under-rigged keel craft, or beamy, sluggish centerboarders designed especially for heavy weather, at sailing localities tending toward light airs. Here, a moderately canvassed, chine-built boat, such as a Blue Jay, younger sister of

Left. The Clamshell, showing the blunt, sawed-off bow characteristic of all prams. (Courtesy, Casco Bay Boats) *Right.* A Hamman Pram demonstrates how even a sizeable man can sail these midget boats, usually measuring 6-10 feet. (Courtesy, R. Hamman & Sons)

the Lightning, might prove the answer. Sporty, intricate racing craft such as Snipes and Firefly Dinghies should be avoided for a year or more. Where winds are stronger and waters more turbulent, a boat along the lines of the Beetle Cat, in which thousands of Cape Cod, Buzzards Bay, and Narragansett Bay youngsters have learned to sail, might well be the selection.

Cat vs. Sloop: This argument has raged from time immemorial, and neither side lacks good ammunition.

Left. The Celebrity, a 19½′ sloop, is available in both keel or centerboard, molded plywood or strip-planked hulls. The latter form of construction glues narrow planks together for strength rather than screwing each plank to ribs. (Courtesy, P. Evanson Boat Co.) *Right.* A fleet of 10′ Dyer Dhows starts a race at the Mystic (Conn.) Seaport Museum. Although manned here by elders, these craft were presented by various yachting organizations (note letters on sails) for use in the Museum's training program for Sea Scouts, Mariners, and other youngsters each summer. (Courtesy, The Anchorage, Inc.)

This writer favors a catboat, preferably along dinghy lines, as best for a beginner, especially when early instruction is supervised. This does not suggest starting in sporty racing dinghies, which can be so lively as to frighten the beginner, or in sluggish, under-rigged, and ultra-safe boats. The cat rig offers a simple boat with a single sail to tend as one learns to steer and balance his craft. The advantage of easy

Left. One of the increasingly popular midget cruisers is the plywood-constructed Corsaire, available at less cost than most popular automobiles. (Courtesy, Nautica Corp.) *Right.* Among the small craft with molded plywood hulls is the Firefly Dinghy, a sporty, planing-hull racer.

handling by a single person enables the new skipper to take a sailing dinghy, or small catboat out alone, after one or two lessons, and practice to his heart's content when the weather is not severe.

In contrast, the sloop almost always demands a crew to tend jib or mainsheet. Most dinghy-type catboats are sufficiently responsive to the helm to keep a skipper alert—important in learning to react quickly to changes in the wind or balance of a boat.

A catboat skipper is close to the water, which permits keeping one eye on his sail and the other on the water in order to visualize quickly the changes of speed brought about by shifts of wind, weight, and the trim of sails. This teaches an understanding of what is happening more easily than when sailing larger or less responsive craft. Moreover, he must learn to do all these things himself without help from instructor or crew. Where weather is more rugged, sturdier catboats may be substituted to produce many of the same results.

Catboats are not the only suitable craft in which to learn sailing, for many famous skippers began their careers in sloops.

Sometimes a sloop may be sailed as a catboat when one is learning, although under such a rig she will not be as well balanced or lively as if designed as a catboat. Aside from numerous sailing and racing dinghies or prams, catboats can be a rarity except in a few localities, and hence new sailors may prefer or need to start in sloops.

A good, though not necessarily conclusive, argument claims that, since sloops are sailed somewhat differently from cats, skippers might do well to start in a type which is more universal for later sailing and racing. The important thing about sailing a sloop is that a skipper must learn the proper balance or adjustment between the trim of jib and mainsail. Once this is mastered, a sloop is a joy to sail. The catboat advocates will retort that jib and mainsail technique is not essential at the very start, and can be easily acquired later. More important to stress is starting in a not-too-sporty boat of moderate size. A few small boats—the recently introduced Sprite is an example—have been designed to sail as either cats or sloops by means of two mast steps, a feature recommending these boats to beginners.

Left. The Flattie, a speedy, hard-chine, shoal-draft centerboarder, which lends herself to home building, dry-sailing and easy maintenance, is very popular on the West Coast, where it's raced by juniors as well as seniors. (Courtesy, International Flattie YRA) *Right.* The 9′ MK Dinghy, a cat-rigged fiberglass dink. (Courtesy, Cape Cod Shipbuilding Co.)

Aside from the cat-sloop controversy, many New Englanders maintain there is no finer boat in which to learn than the dory, a sailing adaptation of the craft used by fishermen of this coast and Nova Scotia, on the fishing banks extending from Newfoundland to Nantucket. The refined racing dory, when not over-canvassed, is a most responsive, lively boat which has produced many fine skippers.

What Price Boats?

Selection of a boat, new or second-hand, will be governed—once the type is determined—by the amount of money the buyer wishes to spend, never losing sight of the factor of maintenance.

Left. The 8′ Plebe, with glass hull and cat rig, is ideal for beginners. (Howard White photo, courtesy, Pearson Corp.) *Right.* Another cat-rigged midget for single-handed sailing is the 8′ fiberglass Feather. (Courtesy, Su-Mark, Inc.)

New Boats: Sailing craft provide a wonderful, healthful recreation, but boats are rated luxury items and hence are not inexpensive. Although the number built increases each year and mass-production is receiving greater attention, a sailboat hull is apt to have a per-foot cost greater than small power craft. This price is exclusive of sails or engines; but, the difference being negligible, a sailboat has the advantage of moving on free air rather than on gas and oil.

Left. Tinker, a 9½′ Turnabout sailed here by New England junior champion Tommy Curtis, Jr. Some 1500 of these have been built in less than a decade for New England and northern New York waters as junior trainers, because their size and rig adapts the craft to early single-handed sailing. (Courtesy, Thomas Curtis, National Turnabout Assn.) **Right.** One of the newer planing-boat classes is the Flying Scot, having a roomy cockpit and ample forward deck. (Courtesy, Gordon Douglass Boat Co., Inc.)

In buying any craft, the emphasis should be to make sure she is safe, sails well, and will not require considerable expenditure immediately. To spend large sums on one's first sailboat is foolish, for the novice should learn to sail in a craft of 8′ to 15′ overall length, which is rugged enough to withstand a bit of hard usage. Frills and bright work will only be banged up.

New craft in the small boat category, which here includes anything roughly under 30′ overall, may be purchased at several price levels. The least expensive are prams and sailing surfboards. The latter—streamlined, watertight boxes with daggerboard and lug or lateen sails—can be tremendous fun with capsizing part of the sport, so their popularity increases in proportion to the warmth of the water. Somewhat tricky to sail, they are not recommended for beginners since the techniques required are different than employed on other boats. They should be sailed close to shore only and by strong swimmers. Prams, despite blunt bows, are essentially dinghies and make good trainers, as the popularity of the Optimist Pram Class has proven by developing good young helmsmen.

The small boat field then expands upward with dinghies, catboats, sloops, day sailers, centerboard and keel racing machines, to small racing cruisers with prices above $6000. The accompanying table, Small Boat Guide, may assist readers in selecting their boat. (See page 122.)

Second-Hand Boats: The used or second-hand boat has advantages as a first craft. With the modern trend to plastics, increasing numbers of satisfactory second-hand boats, at prices considerably less expensive than new craft, may be found on the market. Hence, a second-hand boat, to be replaced by a larger, speedier craft, makes sense for short-term ownership.

A used boat should be looked over carefully before purchase, and here an experienced sailor can offer invaluable advice to the beginner. Wooden boats out of water for prolonged periods may require recaulking—an expensive job or a tedious "do-it-yourself" task—if her seams have opened. Dry rot may be suspected if paint has peeled or a penknife easily enters the wood where sun and circulating air cannot reach. In warm waters only tiny pinholes where bottom paint is scraped away may hint of planking honeycombed inside with passages made by teredos, a marine boring worm. The veteran boatman will want to look, too, for broken ribs or frames.

Less serious but annoying expense or trouble might come from repairs needed to the deck, spars rotting from lack of frequent painting or varnishing, blocks, turnbuckles, and rusted wire rigging requiring replacement. New running rigging is a normal annual or biennial expense, for every true sailor takes pride in having sound, smart, and workable rigging, which prevents accidents. Wholesale replacement of sails might also turn a seeming bargain into "money flowing out the lee scuppers."

The second-hand boat in sound condition, or requiring only nominal expenditure, can save money; for the beginner is bound to give a craft some hard usage while learning. Dents, nicks, paint scraping, and incidental damage will depreciate the value of a new boat much faster than in the case of her used sister. Second-hand craft are especially good for teaching boat maintenance, and every sailor will be a better seaman if he does some of the upkeep himself. Many veteran yachtsmen rarely buy brand new boats, and some second-hand craft remain sound after 50 years of sailing and many changes of ownership.

To summarize, the amount of money a buyer can afford is the first governing factor. The smart newcomer should not splurge until the fundamentals of sailing are learned. Don't be penny-wise and pound-foolish. When buying, remember the economy craft, whether second-hand or new, may fit one's immediate needs far better than the expensive, showy, and deluxe sailboat.

What Will Maintenance Cost?

With preferences of hull design and the "best buy" decided, the prospective boat owner will wish to estimate the cost of equipping and maintenance. This could be vital in the final selection. Into the potpourri of annual maintenance goes hauling, storing, painting, sails, rigging, gear, and accessories— covering items as varied as cushions and trailers, plus perhaps a rowing dinghy, float space, or a club membership. As care of hull can be a big item, a good starting point evolves around whether to buy a wooden planked, plywood, or plastic-hulled craft.

Planked Hull: Only a few wooden sailboats are being built today in the old tradition with either smooth or **lapstrake** (clinker-built or overlapping) planking, but they will be plentiful for many years in the second-hand market. Planked boats, if **well-found** (i.e., soundly built and maintained), are a good buy which, with reasonable care, will last for many years. The maintenance of underbody and topside requires sandpapering to a smooth surface before applying 2 or 3 new coats of paint.

Every 2 or 3 years, even non-racing hulls should be scraped down to bare wood, as painted surfaces deteriorate under constant sun and water exposure. Every fall, underbodies ought to be given one coat of paint, allowed to harden for several months before final coats are applied. Anti-fouling bottom paints are most effective if boats are launched within 24 to 48 hours after painting, while the poisons are most virulent.

The occasional replacement of some caulking may be required, while the deck, cockpit, and interior should have an annual painting. Most owners haul out wooden and plywood boats at least once during the season to clean off marine growth and slime, with perhaps a wet sandpaper rubdown, some painting, and varnishing.

Plywood Hulls: The first major break from traditional planking in yacht construction came when marine sheet plywood was perfected in the late 1930's. Before all problems of its marine use were solved, some sheets warped or separated in wavy effects. Now enduring—numerous early craft have withstood 20 years of hard racing—sheet plywood offers a less expensive form of construction no harder, indeed sometimes easier, to maintain than regularly planked boats.

Following closely the introduction of sheet plywood came molded plywood shapes. This is more satisfactory and permits the compound curves in hulls which sheet plywood precluded even after phenolic resins had improved both kinds. Plywoods, while strong, can be pierced in collisions. Repairs are entirely possible, though molded plywood requires somewhat more expert workmanship. Regular sanding or stripping, and painting, is equally important for plywood and planked hulls. Although plywood still is used widely for new construction, second-hand plywood boats often can be purchased at appealing prices.

Fiberglass Hulls: The buyer thinking of purchasing a new boat should consider fiberglass construction. Initial cost may be higher, but these craft require less maintenance. Many builders are hopeful that initial costs eventually will be reduced to or below the levels of traditionally constructed craft. Fiberglass boats now come with permanent color molded into the hull to alleviate the need for yearly painting. The hulls can be damaged, but often withstand considerable misuse. Owners clever with their hands can make minor repairs. Although fiberglass boats currently are at a premium in the second-hand market, plastic boats of fiberglass, rubber, and other materials will become increasingly available. The tide since 1957 has flowed strongly toward fiberglass among American boat builders. Very few small sailboats are built of aluminum or other metals.

Hauling and Storing: Except in Florida and Southern California, few small sailboats are used year 'round. A strong trend exists everywhere toward **dry-sailing**, which means hauling boats out of water and storing ashore on cradles or trailers between sails. Thus, hauling and storing concerns all boat owners.

When the owner plans to dry-sail or do a major share of his own maintenance, another strong argument is forthcoming for the centerboard boat. They are easy to haul out on beach, ramp, or float, load on a trailer, and take home to back yard, garage, or cellar, where work can be done day or night. Trailers can be borrowed for centerboard boats, whereas those for keel craft are expensive to buy and much harder to rent or borrow. Purchase of a trailer with the boat, especially a racing craft, is wise, permitting the craft to be trailed to home or distant regattas.

Keel boats, with few exceptions, are not easily hauled by amateurs. The simplest method for hauling small keel craft is by crane, hoist, or lift. Installation of electric hoists, which will haul either keel or centerboard boats within specified weight limits, have increased notably in recent years at yacht clubs, municipal facilities, and boatyards. Usually, the charge for their use is moderate.

If an owner plans to haul and store at a boatyard, there may be restrictions concerning any work he does personally on the boat. Some yards permit, others limit, some forbid, and a few charge owners for any personal work. All yards charge for storage and hauling.

Accessories and Extras: The buyer should remember that new boats, like automobiles, have a basic list price, considerably lower than the figure an owner must spend before his craft is ready to sail; many "accessories" actually are necessities. National advertisements often give a factory or f.o.b. price to which a purchaser must add shipping charges.

Another gimmick favored by many dealers is to quote a price and then, in fine print, add "without sails." After freight and sails are included, the buyer may have to purchase necessities such as anchor, rode, pump, life preservers or jackets, boathook, wind pennant, fog horn, oars or paddle—plus extras like hoisting sling, stainless steel rigging, boom vang, outboard bracket, special color or preservative paint jobs, and possibly flotation material. What is furnished and what is extra varies with each builder.

With second-hand craft most items, including sails, come with the boat, but a purchaser should make a check list to ascertain what is included or will need to be bought. Sails of a second-hand boat should be examined carefully by an experienced person to determine whether replacement will be necessary in the near future.

Yearly Maintenance: Besides hauling, storage, and painting expenses, there are other recurring maintenance costs. Running and standing rigging ought to be examined before and during each season to avoid breakage under stress. Spun Dacron rope, while expensive to purchase, has proved durable and economical for running rigging. When wire rigging parts or turnbuckles give way, a spar may break to require costly replacement, and there's always a chance of injury to the crew. Blocks, snaphooks, sail slides, shackles, and winches require checking and replacement from time to time. The smart owner keeps a kit on board for instant replacement of small marine hardware, as well as marline and spare line. Lifejackets, cushions, and bailing equipment may be lost overboard or wear out.

Sails: Sails, along with moorings, rate special maintenance attention. The use of synthetic cloth has reduced the necessity for as frequent sail replacement as existed with cotton sails; yet, new ones will be required from time to time. A sail that has lost its life or drive for racing may still give service for pleasure sailing. Jibs, especially the overlapping variety, tend to wear out sooner than mainsails. While the budget should provide for occasional replacement, periodic examination by a sailmaker to check and repair stitching and damage from chafing may postpone larger expenses.

Mooring: Unless your boat is dry-sailed or kept in a slip with mooring lines, she will need a permanent mooring—this in addition to the anchor which must be kept on board at all times. A heavy non-fouling anchor, mushroom type preferred, or a granite block, is recommended. In mud bottoms, specially poured blocks of cement or other weights are sometimes used, but as owners are protecting an investment with a good mooring they must be leery of taking any risks. Any erring should be toward extra weight and safety.

An iron chain, designed to lie along the bottom, is shackled both to the mooring and a nylon anchor rode whose length depends on the depth of water. The mooring buoy and pennant are attached to the rode. Although nylon does not rot or attract marine borers, both chain and rode should be overhauled yearly to check signs of rust or wear, whether or not the mooring is left in the water year 'round.

Look to the Future: When buying a boat, her future usage should be a consideration. Especially if the prospective sailor is young, eventual enticement into competitive sailing is probable. Hence, when sailboat racing exists in the area, thought should be given to buying a racing-class boat when making a first or second purchase. The boats racing thereabouts should be looked over and a decision made regarding which class appeals to the new owner's needs and capabilities. Many racing boats, extreme racing machines excluded, make good day sailers, and small one-designs of a class raced in your vicinity will have a better resale value than a nondescript craft or class boats not raced locally.

With the foregoing thoughts as a guide, plus some assistance from experienced sailors, the new yachtsman—every pleasure-boat owner is one—should not go far wrong in buying a boat.

Small Boat Guide

The following table, designed to assist readers considering the purchase of boats, lists a number of popular (though by no means all) small boats; i.e., under 30′ overall. They are classified by price range, type, and rig, but such grouping is necessarily arbitrary and tentative. The prices are approximate; the cost of class boats quoted by different builders straddle the classifications (medium price used here). The listing usually is by finished boat price, with sails often—though not always—included. The availability of kits or partially finished boats, at considerably less cost, is noted, but this listing may be incomplete or subject to change. The table is simply a guide and the author cannot be responsible for the complete accuracy of all information.

Dinghies, strictly speaking, are small rowboats, but many today are designed as sailboats. In the lower price classifications dinghies are separated from other types, but larger craft with many characteristics of the dinghy are simply listed as sloops. Most dinghies are cat-rigged, but a few are sloop-rigged as the key in listing will indicate.

KEY: *Available in kits or partially finished.
Italics indicate keel boat.

† Rigged as, or convertible to, cat or sloop.
‡ Keel version of this centerboard boat available.

(C) or (S) indicates catboat or sloop in a classification in which the opposite rig is normal.

UNDER $500 CLASSIFICATION

CATBOATS: Butterball, Merry-Mac.
CATAMARAN: Gunderdink.
DINGHIES: Cape Cod MK, Duckling†, Feather, Grumman, Plebe, Quahog, Royalite, Sprite†, Turnabout.*
PRAMS: Cadet (S)*, Cape Cod, Clamshell, El Toro*, Hamman, Optimist*, Sabot.*
SURFBOARDS: Dixie Scooter, Sailfish*, Sunfish*, Trident.

$500 TO $1000 CLASSIFICATION

CATAMARAN: Lear Cat.*

CATBOATS: Beetle, Duster* (Pram), Interlake MC Scow, Nipper, Woodpussy.

DINGHIES (Cats): Beverly, Cygnet, Dyer Dhow, Dyer Class D, Evanson*†, Interclub, International 12, Lehman Interclub, Lehman 12, Moth*, Penguin*, Snowbird, Tech, Vixen†.

DINGHIES (Sloops): Albacore*, Bantam*, Enterprise*, Firefly*, Flying Dutchman Jr., Jet 14*, Vaurien.

SLOOPS: Blue Jay*, Flattie*, Indian Scout, Lido 14, Ospray, Puffin, Town.

$1000 TO $1500 CLASSIFICATION

CATAMARAN: Gay Cat.

CATBOAT: Hustler.

DINGHIES: Finn (C)*, Filibustier, Gannett, International 14, Jolly Boat*, Thistle.*

SLOOPS: Comet*, Day Sailer, Hampton, Holiday*, Marauder, Mercury (Cape Cod)‡, National One-Design, Rebel, Rocket, Skimmer, Snipe*, Y-Flyer.*

$1500 TO $2000 CLASSIFICATION

CATAMARANS: Shearwater III*, Tiger Cat.

SLOOPS: Celebrity*‡, 5-0-5*, Flying Dutchman*, *Flying 15*, Flying Scot, Hurricane, Indian, Interlake*, Lightning*, Mobjack, *110**, Rhodes 18‡, *SMYRA* (Rhodes 19).

MIDGET CRUISERS: Corsaire (K-CB), Silhouette Mark II.

$2000 TO $2500 CLASSIFICATION

SLOOPS: *Bullseye*, C Scow, D Scow, Highlander*, *Mercury* (San Francisco).

$2500 TO $4000 CLASSIFICATION

SLOOPS: *Atlantic*, Inland Lake E Scow, Raven, *Star**, *210.*

$4000 TO $6000 CLASSIFICATION

CRUISER: Amphibi-Ette* (K-CB).

SLOOPS: *Dragon, Hodgdon 21, Luders 16, Marlin.*

$6000 AND OVER CLASSIFICATION

CRUISERS: Amphibi-Con*(K-CB), Atalanta, Cap Vert (K-CB), Controversy 28*, Junior Holiday‡, New Horizons* (K-CB).

Glossary — A Little Dictionary of Words and Terms Used in Sailing

Many nautical words and terms used in this book are explained in the text. To provide a handy reference, however, as there is no index, this glossary lists and defines those most frequently used.

Abaft. Toward the stern.

Abeam. The direction at right angles to the line of the keel.

Aft. At, toward, or near the stern.

Amidships. The part of a vessel midway from bow to stern, or inboard from her sides.

Backstays. Ropes or wires slanting sharply aft from the mast for the purpose of supporting this spar. Stays requiring adjustment with each change of tack are known as *running backstays* (runners), while one leading directly to the stern is termed a *permanent backstay.*

Ballast. Iron or lead placed low inside a boat to increase stability by lowering the center of gravity. Lead and iron keels are termed outside ballast to distinguish from inside ballast.

Battens. Thin wooden or plastic strips used to hold the leech of a sail and prevent curling. *Batten pockets* hold the battens in sails.

Beam. The greatest breadth, or width, of a vessel.

Beat. A course or action by which a boat sails to windward. *Beating* is sailing to windward by a series of tacks, although the phrase *beating to leeward* is used when a boat sails down the wind on a series of jibes.

Bend. To make a sail fast to a spar or stay by means of groove or track, knots, or snaphooks. To secure with a bend (see Knots).

Bight. A curve in a rope before it becomes a loop. However, the expressions "caught in" or "by a bight" are used when it closes around a limb or object.

Bilge. The turn of the hull below the waterline; also that part inside the hull where bilge water collects above or near keel.

Block. A nautical form of pulley with one or more rollers (sheaves).

Boom. A spar at the foot of a fore-and-aft sail; also a pole used to hold spinnakers outboard.

Bow. The forward part of a vessel. Also, curve of the stem.

Broach. To swing sharply toward the wind when sailing free due to heavy seas, poor steering, etc.

Burdened Vessel. A craft required to keep clear of vessel holding the right of way.

Centerboard. A movable, pivoted device of wood, plastic, or metal, used in place of a keel to give stability, permit sailing in shallower waters than keel craft, and prevent sliding away from wind (leeway). When raised, it is housed in a centerboard trunk. The daggerboard, a sliding form of centerboard which has no pivot, may only be lowered or lifted vertically.

Chain Plates. Metal plates bolted to the side of a boat to which stays are attached to support rigging.

Charts. Nautical maps, giving aids to navigation, water depths, shoals, currents, landmarks, etc.

Chock. A metal casting, usually at the bow, through which mooring and securing lines or ropes are led.

Cleat. A piece of wood or metal with two horns around which ropes are made fast.

Clew. The lower aft corner of a fore-and-aft, or triangular sail.

Close-Hauled. Sailing as close to the wind as possible, with sails trimmed for beating to windward.

Close-Winded. A craft capable of sailing very close to the wind.

Coaming. A raised protection around the cockpit of a small boat.

Cockpit. The undecked portion of a small boat where the helmsman steers and crew sits. It may be a well, usually watertight and sometimes self-bailing, aft of the cuddy or cabinhouse on a keel boat. All other cockpits are called open.

Cringle. A metal or rope eye worked into a clew, tack, or head of a sail for securing purposes.

Cuddy. A decked shelter, less formal than a cabin, usually aft of the mast.

Deadwood. The solid timbers between keel and hull proper.

Downhaul. A rope or tackle by which a sail is pulled downward, usually to improve its shape.

Draft. The depth of water needed to float a boat.

Dry Sailing. When boats are stored ashore on trailers or cradles between each use, or transported overland from port to port to race or cruise.

Ease. To relieve pressure on sail or helm—to pay out a sheet, to luff, etc.

Fairlead. An eye or fitting which changes the direction of a sheet or rope led through it. Many boats have adjustable fairleads.

Fall. The hauling part of a rope; also, the standing part.

Fetch. When a craft sailing to windward can make its objective without another tack.

Fin. A thin projection from the underbody for steadying and stability purposes. In sailboats, usually a narrow, deep keel—often of metal—with bulbous section at bottom.

Fly. Usually a masthead pennant, pointer, or windsock to assist skipper in determining *apparent wind* direction as related to boat, which may not be exactly the same as *true wind* direction. Bits of yarn tied to rigging for same purpose.

Foot. Lower edge of a sail. *Forefoot* is where stem joins keel.

Fore-and-Aft. The rig used on most small sailboats—technically, in line with, parallel to keel.

Foremast. The forward mast of a schooner (see diagram of rigs).

Frames. The ribs to which planking is attached, with sometimes a fine distinction made between ribs and heavier, less numerous frames interspersed between series of ribs.

Free. Sailing with the wind anywhere from abeam to due aft. Also means to cast off, untangle, permit to run easily.

Freeboard. Vertical distance from waterline to deck.

Gaff. Spar hoisted on aft side of mast to support head of a sail, hence *gaff-rigged.*

Garboard (strake). Plank nearest to keel.

Genoa. A large, overlapping jib.

Gooseneck. A metal fitting, normally a universal joint, securing boom to mast.

Gudgeon. An eye fitting to hold *pintles* of a rudder.

Guy. A rope or wire used to steady or support.

Halyard (also *Halliard or Haliard*). Rope or wire used to hoist sails.

Hard-a-lee. Final command used in tacking a boat, i.e. coming about.

Head. Upper corner of sail. Also a boat's toilet. *Headboard* is a wooden, plastic, or metal fitting at head of sail.

Headstay. Usually the forward stay supporting a mast, sometimes called *forestay,* but some boats have both.

Head-to-wind. With bow headed into wind and sails shaking.

Headway. Forward motion of a boat.

Heave. To throw, but also to haul in or upon. *Heave-to,* lying with a boat's bow held head-to-wind.

Heel. The tilt, tip, list, heeling, or laying-over of a boat, usually due to wind.

Helm. The tiller or wheel used to steer a boat. With tillers, to put *helm down* turns toward wind as in tacking, *helm up* away from as in jibing. *Helmsman,* one who steers.

Hike. To climb or to lean out to windward to counteract excessive heeling.

Hull. The main body of a boat as distinct from spars, sails, and gear.

In stays or *in irons.* When head-to-wind while tacking. When a craft remains in stays unduly long with no way she is *In Irons.*

Jib. A triangular sail set forward of mainmast on a small boat, of foremast on schooner. The inner of two jibs is a *forestaysail.*

Jibe or *Gybe.* To change tacks by turning away from the wind with the boom shifting from one side to the other (see also Beating).

Jib-head or *Jib-headed.* A tall rig with triangular mainsail, often miscalled Marconi. *Bermudian rig* is perfectly correct.

Jibstay. The forward stay on which jib is hoisted.

Jigger. The shorter, aft mast of a yawl or ketch.

Jumper Strut. A single or forked strut for added support placed aloft on forward side of a mast.

Keel. The lowest permanent part of the hull, hence the backbone of a boat. In keel yachts it extends deep below the rest of the hull. In centerboard boats, it is the central timber through which the board lowers (see Fin).

Knee. A timber with two arms connecting frames and beams to give added strength.

Knot. A measure of speed, one nautical mile per hour. The tying or securing of rope to objects or other rope, including the tying of loops in a rope. For specific *knots, bends, hitches,* and *turns,* see Chapter 14, *"Basic Knots."*

Lay. Of a rope, the direction of the twist of yarns, or other fiber parts in the making of *strands, ropes,* and *cables.* To *lay,* same as to *Fetch.*

Lazarette. A small enclosed space under the deck near stern.

Lee or *Leeward.* Away from the direction of the wind, hence *lee* side, and to *leeward. Lee shore,* against which the wind is blowing. *Lee* or *leeward helm,* unbalanced condition which turns the boat's bow away from the wind. *Lee bow,* an object off the bow to leeward or a force against the bow from leeward, *lee bow tide. In the lee,* behind the boat, land, or object to windward. *By the lee,* running to leeward with the wind and boom on the same side.

Leech. The aft edge of a fore-and-aft or triangular sail.

Light Sails. Spinnakers and other sails of light materials used to increase boat's speed off the wind.

Lines. General term for light ropes, also used for any running rigging. Drawings showing the shapes of hulls.

Luff. The forward edge of a fore-and-aft sail. The shaking of a sail when a boat points too high for her trim. The spilling of wind from a sail. To turn toward the wind, the first action in tacking, or for tactical and sheet-trimming purposes.

Mainmast. The principal mast of a sloop, catboat, yawl, or ketch; the taller aft mast of a two-masted schooner.

Mainsail. The triangular, fore-and-aft sail set on the aft side of a mainmast.

Mainsheet. The rope by which a boom or sail is pulled in or slacked off, usually through a system of blocks.

Marconi. A tall mast used with the jib-headed or Bermudian rig. *Not a rig.*

Mast. A vertical spar supporting sails and rigging. See *Main, Fore,* and *Mizzen* masts.

Mizzen. The small aft mast on a yawl or ketch. See also *Jigger.*

Mooring. The relatively permanent anchor or weight to which a yacht rides by means of chain, rope, and pennant, when not sailing. *To moor* is to pick up a *mooring buoy* and secure to a mooring.

Offshore. Away from, or a wind blowing off, the shore.

Off the Wind. Sailing on any course except to windward.

On the Wind. Close hauled.

Outboard. Beyond a boat's side or hull.

Outhaul. A line used to secure the *clew* of a sail.

Overstand. To go beyond an objective, usually unintentionally.

Painter. A short piece of rope securing the bow of a boat to a landing or other object.

Parachute. A spinnaker cut so as to resemble a parachute.

Part. To break. Also, the hauling, standing, or running part of a rope.

Pay Off, Pay Out. A boat *pays off*

when her bow turns away from the wind. *Pay out* is to slacken.

Pennant. A small, narrow flag. A wire or rope by which a mooring is attached to the boat.

Pinch. To sail a boat so close to the wind that her sails shake or her progress slows.

Pintle. A metal, pin-like fitting allowing a rudder to swing when inserted in the *gudgeon.*

Point, Pointing. To head high, rather close to the wind.

Port. The left side of a boat when looking forward. *Port Tack,* when the wind blows over the port side.

Privileged Vessel. A vessel holding the right of way, required to hold her course.

Quarter. The part of a boat's side aft of *abeam* and forward of the *stern.*

Rail. The outer edge of the deck.

Rake. The inclination of a mast from the vertical.

Rap Full. With all sails drawing full, just a little off the wind.

Reach, Reaching. All sailing courses between close-hauled and running. *Close reach,* sailing nearly close-hauled with sheets just *eased. Beam reach,* sailing with the wind *abeam. Broad reach,* sailing with the wind *abaft the beam* and with sails well out on the *quarter.*

Ready About. Preparatory order when tacking.

Reeve. To pass rope, sheet, or halyard through block, fairlead, etc.

Rib. See *Frame.*

Ride. To lie at anchor. *Hove-to* in a storm (ride out).

Rig. The character of a boat's mast and sail arrangement. *Jib-head* rig, *gaff* rig, *cat* rig, etc. See diagram in text on page 7.

Rigging. The wires and ropes of a boat. *Standing rigging* supports spars. *Running rigging* sets or trims sails.

Roach. The outward curve of the *leech* of a sail.

Rode. Anchor line of a small boat.

Run, Running. To sail almost directly before the wind. The aft underwater part of a boat's hull is called *run.*

Seaway. Place where rough or moderate seas are running. A well traveled waterway.

Secure. To make fast.

Set. The shape of a sail. The direction of tide. The pushing of a boat to *leeward* of its course. *Set up,* or *taut,* to take in, take up, usually in order to relieve strain, or improve shape of a sail.

Shackle. A U-shaped metal fitting with a pin or screw across the open end used to join halyards and ropes to sails or other objects.

Sheave. The wheel in a block.

Sheer. The curve of the deck between bow and stern. *Sheer off,* to bear away. *Sheer strake,* topmost plank on the side of a boat.

Shrouds. Wires or ropes supporting mast. Also, supporting bowsprits and outriggers.

Skeg. An extension or protrusion of the keel aft, usually to aid steering or support an outboard rudder.

Skipper. Person in command. In sailing, skipper is often used interchangeably with *helmsman.*

Slip. To cast off. Also, a mooring area between small piers or floating booms.

Spar. General term for masts, booms, gaffs, etc.

Spinnaker. A light sail used when running and reaching, and held out from the mast by a *spinnaker boom* or *pole.*

Spreader. A horizontal strut to which shrouds or stays are attached, to support the mast and spread rigging.

Starboard. The right side of a boat when looking forward. A boat sails on *starboard tack* when the wind blows over starboard side.

Stays. Ropes and wires supporting masts. *Shrouds* are special stays, usually on each side of mast. See also *Backstay, Forestay, Jibstay, Headstay.*

Stem. The foremost timber at the bow of a boat. Stems may be plastic or metal.

Stern. The aft extremity of a boat. See Chapter 2, Hull section, for types.

Strake. Any plank on the side or bottom of a hull. See *Garboard* and *Sheer* strakes.

Tack. The forward lower corner of a fore-and-aft or triangular sail. A boat under way sails on a *tack,* either starboard or port. For example, *starboard tack* when the wind blows over her starboard side. A boat *tacks* when she changes from *starboard* to *port* tack or vice versa by turning toward the wind. She is then said to have made a *tack.*

Taut. Stretched tight, snug.

Tender. A sailboat lacking sufficient stability, opposite of stiff. Also a dinghy-type craft which may be rowed or sailed.

Thwarts. Seats that go across, *thwartship,* the cockpit of a small boat.

Tiller. A wooden bar or rod used to steer small boats by fitting to the top of the rudder or rudder-post. Called "stick" at times. Tiller extensions are known also as *hiking sticks.*

Topsides. Usually the sides of the boat lying between waterline and rail. In a broad sense, any above-water part of the hull.

Transom. Usually applied to mean a broad stern that is a straight or almost vertical line from the deck to the water. It may be planked, a single board, or molded. Loosely, transom is sometimes used almost interchangeably with stern. A long stern tapering from the waterline to the sternboard is called a *counter* or yacht stern.

Traveller. Metal rod on which sheet blocks slide athwartships for sail-trimming purposes. Rope or wire travellers are technically *bridles.*

Trim. To set sails correctly in relation to the wind by means of sheets. The fore-and-aft balance of a boat. Also used in relation to *thwartship* balance, i.e., with *heeling* and *hiking.*

Tuning. The delicate adjustment of a boat's rigging, sails, and hull to the proper balance which assures the best sailing performance.

Turnbuckle. A threaded link which pulls 2 eyes together for setting up standing rigging.

Vang. A wire or a rope used to steady a spar—most common usage, boom vang.

Veer. A shift of the wind in a clockwise direction, or toward the stern. The wind may *haul* aft or clockwise, however. When the wind shifts counterclockwise, it *backs.*

Wake. The foamy disturbed water left astern by a moving boat.

Waterline. Where a boat floats in the water when properly trimmed, the division line between underbody and topsides. Often a distinctive painted stripe called the *boot-topping* or *top.*

Way. Movement through the water. A boat's forward way is *headway;* backward, *sternway;* and any movement, *underway,* especially immediately after leaving a mooring or landing.

Weather. A synonym for *windward.*

Well Found. A well-equipped boat with all gear in good condition.

Whisker-Pole. A light pole or stick used to pole out a jib to *windward* to permit sailing *wing-and-wing* on a run, when a spinnaker is not set.

Winch. A small drum-shaped mechanical device, similar to a windlass, to increase hauling power on sheets and halyards.

Windward. Toward the wind, hence the *weather* side of a boat, and *to windward. Windward* and *weather* are almost interchangeable in speaking of *windward shore, weather bow,* and *windward helm. A weather helm* is one which tends to turn the boat's bow toward the wind, a desirable feature if not too strong. See *Lee and Leeward.*

Wing-and-Wing. When jib and mainsail, or any two working sails of a boat are trimmed from the opposite sides.

Working Sails. The ordinary fore-and-aft sails, such as jib and mainsail, exclusive of light sails or storm sails.

Yacht. Any craft, regardless of size, used for pleasure, from a rowboat to Her Majesty Queen Elizabeth's *Britannia.*

Yaw. The side-to-side, off-course swinging of a boat due to steering badly in a *seaway.*